The Recovery of Purpose

THE RECOVERY
OF PURPOSE

ÉMILE CAILLIET

H | B

HARPER & BROTHERS PUBLISHERS
NEW YORK

Library of Congress catalog card number: 59–14530

This book is dedicated to
the Brotherhood of those who
are heavy laden

CONTENTS

CONTENTS

III

POINTS OF CONTACT BETWEEN
MODERN SCIENCE AND THEOLOGY

IV

THE PROMETHEAN CHARACTER OF
A COMMON PLIGHT

ACKNOWLEDGMENTS

It is a pleasant duty to express my gratitude for permission to quote from the following publications: Herbert L. Samuel, *Essays in Physics,* New York: Harcourt, Brace and Company, Inc., 1952; *Collected Papers of Evelyn Underhill,* edited by Lucy Menzies, New York: Longmans, Green and Company, Inc., 1946; E. N. Mozley, *The Theology of Albert Schweitzer for Christian Inquirers,* New York: The Macmillan Company, 1950; Albert Schweitzer, *The Mysticism of Paul the Apostle,* New York: The Macmillan Company, 1955; William Temple, *Nature, Man and God,* New York: The Macmillan Company, 1934; D. M. Baillie, *God Was in Christ,* New York: Charles Scribner's Sons, 1948; Bertrand Russell, *A History of Western Philosophy,* New York: Simon and Schuster, 1945; W. T. Stace, "Man Against Darkness," in *The Atlantic Monthly* (Sept. 1948); Paul S. Minear, *Eyes of Faith,* Philadelphia: The Westminster Press, 1946; Charles Hartshorne, *The Divine Relativity,* New Haven: Yale University Press, 1948.

E.C.

INTRODUCTION

THE modern mood and method so easily identified with "science" has brought about a loss of the ultimate purpose which heretofore had testified to the finality of the Christian world view. This naturally suggests the thought that only a reconceived Christianity can cope with the resulting plight. Yet the sense of futility which has overwhelmed our age is heightened by a widespread impression that there can be no such healing reconception. Christianity, it is claimed, is steadily losing meaning and significance among our contemporaries. The reason this fact is not as yet universally acknowledged, it is further argued, is that vestigial structures are periodically reanimated in well-staged gatherings, and perpetuated by warmed-over theological titles and well-financed periodicals. The total effect of these and similar activities, according to this pessimistic diagnosis, would seem to amount to a cultivation of obsolescence. In their anxiety to remain intellectually honest, a large section of our contemporaries will have no part in "backward" steps involving the surrender of modernity's best-assured advances. And so, what Gustav Fechner called "the night view"[1] is said to be here to stay, all wishful thinking to the contrary notwithstanding.

The most distressing feature in the attitude just outlined is that it generally ignores a promise of genuine rebirth now silently coming to expression in the labors of love of a dedicated Christian scholarship, as well as—and this is the wonder of it all—in the very achievements of modernity itself. And just as the birth and human career of Jesus Christ took place in a display of power through humility and weakness, the renaissance now at hand awaits the fullness of time in unheralded advances toward reconciliation and wholeness.

These pages aim at a clarification of the resulting situation with a view to helping men of goodwill find their bearings, and more proficiently proceed with the task of relating their efforts to proper ends. This they would attempt in a spirit of submission to fact. William Ernest Hocking has insistently drawn attention to a striking analogy between Bacon's formulation of the principle of inductive observation, and the Lord's disclosure of the fundamental paradox of the Christian life. Said Bacon, "We cannot command nature except by obeying her." The statement of Jesus was, "He that loseth his life for my sake shall find it." Our Lord's disclosure further suggests that the truth can be reached only through surrender of anthropocentric ways of thinking, together with ever-increasing submission to the ways of God which are not our ways.

Right at this point there comes to light one of the many lessons Christianity needs to learn from modernity. Modernity consistently proceeds upon Bacon's dictum, while Christianity easily yields to the temptation of taking liberties with the Lord's disclosure and its implications. As a result modernity may be said to have advanced farther and more efficiently in the knowledge of nature, than Christianity in the knowledge of the Creator and his ways. Consensus of views is the criterion and aim in the scientific realm, whereas confusion of tongues and bitter contention too often characterize Christian self-assertion in the theological realm. The formula, "It seemed good to the Holy Spirit and to us . . ." has too often preluded heresy hunting and the fires of persecution. We no longer burn heretics, but a number of hardly veiled substitutes for the practice have been devised. Self-examination is in order on our part, together with a mending of our ways, if we expect to secure a hearing from those to whose condition we should address ourselves.

In this connection, no individual Christian or body of Christians is exempt from blame. Neither may any individual Christian or body of Christians assume a monopoly on truth. If it be said that there exists a dividing line among Christians, the same can hardly set "evangelicals" so-called apart from "liberals." Any "liberal" worth his salt knows that Christianity is essentially concerned with the Evangel. An objective consideration of the total picture is more likely to reveal a dividing line among men who have laid their hand to the plow, between those who look back with nostalgic longings on the one hand, and on the other, those who look ahead in the obedience of faith. I imply that the distinction is between those who hark back to the ready-made solutions of ages gone by, and those who look forward to ever more accurate and constructive patterns of understanding. This they do in the awareness that the Word of God cannot be identified with any degree of anthropomorphic formulating, however hallowed the formulation. As it was said of old, knowledge begins with wonder. Those who claim to have knowledge in its once-for-allness rarely learn anything new. Should they perchance be confronted by fresh information, their impression likely would be that they had lost something. Their next natural move would be to expose as destructive the creative activity which threatened their peace of mind—a peace of mind in this case comparable to the peace of the grave.

To speak of a Christian recovery of purpose then is to speak of an emergence from obsolete interpretations. This does not imply in the least that understanding should be given priority over profession and commitment. It is only that sanity goes a long way toward making for sanctity, the alternative being an unbearable strain on Christian life and practice. The Christian intellect should act as an incentive, not as an inhibitor. Still less should its activity be summed up in the perpetuation of roadblocks into monuments to the glory of an ill-conceived deity. For such is the type of activity which prevents our age from heeding and gaining access to the realities involved in evangelical Christianity.

A treatment along these lines admittedly remains open to the danger of assuming that the God who was and is in Christ is in any way bound by circumstances as we figure them out. I had just begun to realize this when my two-year-old granddaughter made me fearful lest I should be carried away by my anxiety to drive home a strictly logical argument. She suddenly interrupted her game to listen to a recording of Handel's *Messiah*. Having listened intently for a while she began to dance to one of the most inspiring passages. Then she rushed to her little bed and fetched back her illustrated book on God which accompanies her to sleep every night.

Truly God is the great Doer of the unexpected, his wonders to perform. Whatever part those who are his co-laborers may feel inspired to play in his service, remains forever that of unprofitable servants. Who am I that I should expose with any finality the seeming inadequacy of such or such a form of evangelism?

It is with this awe-inspiring feeling of personal inadequacy and humility before God, that I turn to the task at hand.

PART I

Is There Room for Purpose in the Scientific World?

PART 1

1

The Drama of Cosmic Purpose

THIS world has always been in need of salvation, and never more so than it is today. For it is a fact that our age has lost the sense of ultimate purpose gained over thousands of years of human life and thought. In so doing we have reverted to that sense of doom which prevailed in ancient cultures and still characterizes contemporary primitive societies.

We seem to have conquered doom, and this mostly thanks to the Gospel, only once more to fall prey to doom; nay, to more virulent, more disheartening forms of doom. It is as if the looping of the loop had been sealed in our time, and modern man had reverted to the ancient cave. The point, however, is that it would not any longer be the same cave, but a darker one. Neither would the new caveman be the caveman his forefather used to be, for he could not conjure the aching vision of the liberation intervening generations had known.

Let us pause on this crucial aspect, because the first concern of Christianity always has been for the people who sit in darkness—in the present situation, a darkness all the more awful because it remembers the great light that failed.

What gives meaning to human existence is a sense of purpose: "Is there a meaning to it all?" Most people have asked the question in a mood of dejection on occasions when they had lost faith in the relevance of some endeavor. At such times they were overwhelmed by the apparent futility of their best intentions. They spoke of "giving up the attempt"—perhaps a whole undertaking heretofore deemed worthy of sustained effort. In more tragic circumstances a nervous breakdown may have intervened, or even the thought of suicide. Extreme forms of discouragement are detected by depth psychology in generalized, mostly unconscious states where the disheartening process actually amounts to surrender of the will-to-live. Authorities in the field describe this condition in the seemingly tautological aphorism that an individual dies when he no longer cares to live. Thus after long doubts and vacillations Sigmund Freud decided to assume the existence of only two basic instincts, Eros, or the creative instinct on the one hand, and on the other the destructive instinct sometimes called Thanatos, after the Greek god of death.

It already has appeared that there are degrees of gravity in loss of purpose. There are brief, almost incidental instances which may be likened to mere ripples on the surface of existence. For instance, we make elaborate preparations for the visit of a friend. He gets up late and misses the train. Our sense of futility in a case like this is not likely to last long. More grievous may be the dereliction of trusted fellow workers, bringing to nought an elaborate plan. Supposing now that years of dedicated effort should end in dismal failure, we may be led to question the very ground of our dedication. Indeed, the work of a lifetime may ultimately prove to have missed the mark to the point of giving the lie to the purposeful outlook one has firmly and consistently held. Such gradation in the preceding illustrations suggests that the issue of purpose is raised all the more forcefully as the range is extended and the perspective amplified, until the issue becomes that of cosmic purpose. Frederic W. H. Myers no doubt had the latter version in mind when he said that, should he ever get the chance of putting a question to the Sphinx, he would ask, "Is the universe friendly?"

The issue of cosmic purpose is the crucial issue we must face to reach any worth-while conclusion regarding the meaning of life. Supposing you or I were put on our mettle, we would naturally want to ask the question of all questions, that in which our whole destiny is at stake. We would want to know whether or not the sacred horror of Oedipus King of Thebes were to be our lot. With a dreadful fate hovering over him ever since the oracle had spoken, his obsession had been with the inevitable.

> 'twill come! 'twill come!

the seer had uttered with a sense of doom. Does this fatalistic utterance apply to our own situation? Are we but pawns in the blind hands of fate? But more. Now that fate has become destiny in the Christian climate of our Western world, is it at all thinkable that we should revert to the doom of pagans? And what a doom that would be, to believe that on this human scene where Jesus Christ died, life

> is a tale
> Told by an idiot, full of sound and fury,
> Signifying nothing.[1]

Or, in the words of James Thomson's *The City of Dreadful Night,* that

> None can pierce the vast black veil uncertain
> Because there is no light beyond the curtain;
> . . . all is vanity and nothingness.[2]

Truly the drama of modern man is the drama of cosmic purpose, and an awful drama it proves to be to one who takes the long view of it. I have just pointed out that the ancients, very much in the manner of our contemporary primitives, labored under a sense of doom ultimately destined to be overcome through the glory of the Gospel; and further, that it would seem that a sense of cosmic purpose emerged in the Christian Era, only to fall prey to more virulent, more disheartening forms of doom. Yet I would draw further attention to some of the baleful aspects of that relapse.

What used to be a "Pilgrim's Progress" has become in our time a "Long Day's Journey into Night." As Eugene O'Neill's posthumous drama unfolds—and the story practically tells itself—there is progressively forced upon us the notion that events work of their own accord, successive happenings being purely derivative in a purposeless universe. Once we learn about antecedents we are led to wonder how anything could have turned out differently. However one may deplore the outcome, every occurrence that irresistibly leads to it is apprehended as necessitated by what Lucretius called the nature of things. At no time is there a hint that God may intervene to guide anyone or ordain anything to some providential end. There is no room for Providence in this pattern of fate and doom. And this is fatalism in a new key—a fatalism all the more tragic because it reasserts itself in a Christian climate. It is noteworthy, moreover, that the play has taken the public by storm in Europe as well as on Broadway, and this not through sheer scandal-mongering stirred up by the autobiographical character of the drama. Neither should we credit the success essentially to the undeniable qualities of the play. The main element in that success is that the plot and the naturalness of its unfolding speak to the condition of our contemporaries. We know only that which we are. The common substance of the spectators' woes as epitomized by one of the leading dramatists of our age provides the *catharsis* they so badly crave. *Long Day's Journey into Night* truly completes the looping of the loop initiated by Sophocles in the sacred horror of *Oedipus King of Thebes*. In its own way our uprooted intelligentsia echoes afresh the outcry, "God is dead."

Our question now is: how did our modern world revert to this aggravated pagan version of a purposeless, meaningless world whose motions are at the mercy of blind forces, and this in spite of nearly two thousand years of Christian life? At this juncture also a detailed, searching analysis would be in order, and it is my fervent hope that the problem may increasingly draw the attention of specialists. What strikes the general observer, however, is that the main foundation for the new view has been laid by modernity in general, and by modern science in particular, and this feature will hold our interest throughout these pages.

Briefly stated, the main fact is that modernity has been increasingly wary of finality and purpose. Purposiveness again and again has appeared to the scientist as an intruder and troublemaker, and science seems to have progressed in the measure as it dispensed with it. And pray, why should science take it into consideration at all? Such popular and hardly impressive answers as that of Alex Comfort, the English poet-scientist, need not retain us for long. God's working in the universe is not only inscrutable, he argues, but so well concealed that the unconvinced student is unable to detect any vestige of observable material relating to it. More weighty are Bertrand Russell's views on the subject, as expressed in his essay, *A Free Man's Worship*,[3] because they are undergirded by a scholarship which later culminated in the three-volume publication with Alfred North Whitehead of *Principia Mathematica*,[4] and paved the way for subsequent developments in symbolic logic. Russell's profession of faith constitutes in effect a statement of his conclusions, and of what he sees to be their implications for an enlightened man's life and conversation. To him, then, man is the product of blind and meaningless causes. His origin, his growth, his hopes, fears, loves and beliefs are merely the outcome of accidental collocations of atoms. No fire, no heroism, no intensity of thought and feeling may be said to point to an individual existence beyond the grave. All human values and achievements, even the brightness of human genius at its best, are destined to total extinction in the vast death of a universe in ruins.

There are those who may detect an aching note of stoic despair in such bravado. However this may be, the dominating impression is that the advances of modernity have implied a calculated surrender of purpose as a Christian culture had formulated it, or implied it in its creeds and statements of "fundamentals" down to our day. All that would seem to be left of Purpose with a capital P is a convenient psychological term which, according to Julian Huxley, suggests a mere anthropomorphic projection of our ways of thinking into the economy of nature.

The reader may rightly object at this juncture that the rank and file care little about such conclusions, in fact, know nothing whatsoever about them. Is not the man in the street more concerned about the rising cost of living, the standing of his favorite baseball team in the American or in the National League, not to speak of the next movie or television feature? I agree—and yet with the further remark that any such ignorance or indifference may be as much a part of the total picture as the statement of the scholar. The over-all view which now forces our attention permeates the whole human fabric. And incidentally, both movies and television play a large part in communicating to the rank and file the outlook on life implied in our loss of purpose. They, like the theater, the press, or even the most casual conversations, unconsciously convey the view of a senseless, purposeless, meaningless world of matter in motion.

There are those finally—and I have left them for the end because I am reluctant to reprove—who will pass a blanket judgment on the proponents of the purposeless view and ascribe their blindness to sinful pride. "Blind leaders of the blind" may be their summation of such "hopeless cases" as those of Bertrand Russell and Julian Huxley. I may even have been condemned by now for having paid so much attention to "reprobates."

This however will not do. Such self-righteous attitudes simply ignore the facts. They amount to a sweeping condemnation of a multitude of some of the most progressive, most productive scholars of our day and age, and of research methods wrought out in the midst of the greatest difficulties. Above all, they amount to a blank dismissal of men of goodwill who in their own way echo Luther's "I cannot otherwise," their alternative as they see it being double-mindedness and hypocrisy. Such men, I have said, are no longer burned at the stake. Should one then have recourse in their case to character assassination, further disposing of those who echo their views by some pronouncement of guilt through association? The new inquisitors had better look up Rufus Jones's *The Church's Debt to Heretics*[5] before they do anything of the sort.

The issue was brought to a head a few years ago when an article by Professor W. T. Stace of Princeton entitled "Man Against Darkness" appeared in *The Atlantic Monthly* and aroused a fury of debate in itself significant. Here was the frank public confession of a highly respected scholar who hardly concealed his grief at seeing forced upon us all the disheartening view of a dark, dead universe completely indifferent to us. Characterizing the notion of purpose, he rightly connected it with causation, the emphasis being on finality: "The final cause of a thing or event," he explained, "meant the purpose it was supposed to serve in the universe, its cosmic purpose." Now that science in its most remarkable achievements had eliminated any kind of recourse to purpose, we were confronted with a nature summed up in motions of matter governed by blind forces and laws. Hence there could

[23]

not be any ideal, moral or otherwise, in the world outside us. Then, with a most penetrating insight came the thrust—a diagnosis which every earnest Christian should heed:

It is this which has killed religion. Religion could survive the discoveries that the sun, not the earth, is the center; that men are descended from simian ancestors; that the earth is hundreds of millions of years old. These discoveries may render out of date some of the details of older theological dogmas, may force their restatement in new intellectual frameworks. But they do not touch the essence of the religious vision itself, which is the faith that there is a plan and purpose in the world. . . . The essential religious spirit . . . cannot survive destruction of belief in a plan and purpose of the world, for that is the very heart of it. Religion can get on with any sort of astronomy, geology, biology, physics. But it cannot get on with a purposeless and meaningless universe.

If the scheme of things is purposeless and meaningless, then the life of man is purposeless and meaningless too. Everything is futile, all effort is in the end worthless.[6]

What a precious pointer, this! Shall we then expose the professor's "infidelity," or rather learn from him and proceed upon what we have learned?

What then do we learn? Essentially this: it is true that the plight of modern man must be ultimately ascribed to a loss of his sense of cosmic purpose. For this loss, the very methods which have brought about the remarkable advances of modern science are responsible. Yet according to Professor Stace, that which has been lost may not be purpose as such, but rather "the final cause of a thing or event" as understood in terms of *the purpose it was supposed to serve* in the universe." My further emphasis is of course on the word "supposed."

Who was responsible for the possibly gratuitous assumptions implied in that word "supposed"? Was it the Word of God? Or was it a theology using the conceptions devised especially by Greek formulators of causality, chief of whom is Aristotle, the formulator of the four classical causes? Let us keep this question in mind. It may turn out to prove a useful pointer in this inquiry.

We are now in a position to evaluate better the situation which confronts a Christian as he comes to grips with the contemporary situation. Whatever may have been the cycle of circumstances which have brought about the sense of futility we detect in the world today, are the detractors of purpose actually *sure* that this new darkness which has fallen upon men and overwhelmed them is here to stay? If it be, they need to know; for no one cares to live in a fool's paradise, however enticing it may prove to be. A man would rather steel himself and strive to emulate the stoicism of those noble souls who have accepted their fate, and henceforth live to serve their fellow men with an impressive dignity. On the other hand, should the new darkness prove to be merely the aftermath of a premature dismissal of the case, they need to be made aware of that also. Why otherwise should they be allowed to lead an ultimately meaningless life strained by overexertion, within the confines of an arbitrarily limited horizon? If it be said even that their call is to the stoical life, why should they not consider Christianity, that stoicism of the poor?

Such is their intellectual honesty, however, that they are likely to heed only a kind of approach which does not involve on their part the surrender of those undeniable advances of modernity which they have learned to value so highly.

2

Twilight of the Final Cause

WE HAVE seen that the notion of purpose was identified with that of final cause, and that accordingly the twilight of the one implied the twilight of the other. So great is the impact of this diagnosis that we need now to consider further its relevance.

We would first realize that secular thinking originally formulated its own notion of purpose. It is a fact that it did so in terms of causality with special attention to the final cause. It should therefore be agreed that the secular version of purpose can be best interpreted in the context of the history of the idea of cause.

The method of reasoning by the cause was originated in philosophy by Plato in the *Meno.* He further developed the notion of formal cause in the *Philebus,* and that of efficient cause in the *Timaeus.* It was at this point that Aristotle undertook a further systematization of causality. This he did by considering that in our world of concrete reality there is no form, that is, no exemplification of the total character which constitutes an intelligible structure, without a substratum of matter. Matter, as he saw it, is constantly striving for a goal which implies completion. Hence a basic view of causality according to which form is actualized in matter. The bird, for instance, is the actuality of the egg. There seems to be at work in nature a kind of blueprinting according to which things always proceed in this manner. Hence, an element of finality calling for the actualization of forms in matter, as is the case when a statue may be said to have called forth its shape out of a mass of brass. In this case, brass constituted the *material* cause. To be sure, it took an artist to make the statue. He may therefore be considered as the *efficient* cause of the process. The "blueprint" he followed acted as the *formal* cause. The finished statue proves to have been the *final* cause. And so we empirically detect at our human level these four causes at work—namely, the material cause, the efficient cause, the formal cause, and the final cause.

Let us realize that this kind of systematization is all the more plausible, all the more tempting and satisfying, as it implies from beginning to end empirical observation at our own level in terms of our own anthropomorphic make-up. A resulting sense of familiarity with what is common to us all may account for the perennial character of these Aristotelian views, another factor being the further implication of uniformity in the processes of nature. And because of this doubly satisfying character, we readily see how natural it was for a Church craving stability to hold on to such views once they had provided the most convenient means of expressing the Christian faith.

This is what actually happened when Aristotle's ultimate matterless form faded away into the Thomistic Pure Act of existence henceforth identified with the God of the Bible, and upon whom (or should I perchance say, upon which?) every particular element depended for its existence. This Pure Act *was* the Prime Mover, the First Cause, the Principle and End of all design and purposiveness in the universe. Henceforth a Christianized Aristotle provided the necessary clues to the relation of God to his creation, as well as of the soul to the body, to the point that detecting the resulting harmonies of nature transfigured the life of the mind into an act of worship. Truly a magnificent conception, a vision hard to surrender whether we think of it in totality or with reference to the endless possibilities of its corollaries.

And yet this is the conception, this is the vision which modern science has felt constrained to surrender under the strain of what Whitehead has called "irresistible and stubborn facts." This process of surrender involved profound transformations of the Aristotelian view of causality. Not only were scientific advances responsible for these transformations, but so was the clarification of the biblical knowledge of God ushered in by the Reformation. The first two causes eliminated were the final cause and the material cause, and this in the wake of "the golden age of science," namely, the seventeenth century. Only two of the Aristotelian causes were left, the formal cause and the efficient cause. Already with Descartes, however, then with Spinoza and Leibnitz, these two were so closely united that they were well on their way to fusing into one efficient cause increasingly identified with the "reason" offered for the effects observed in phenomena. It should be carefully noted that this view of causality was not without analogy to the Reformers' view of God's agency. Malebranche was not far from it when he ascribed all efficacy to God. Yet by then, mostly under the influence of John Locke, the context had become empirical, and it was in that context that David Hume dealt the final blow at what remained of the Aristotelian view of causality. With the deftness of the meat carver of Plato's *Phaedrus*, he aimed his thrust at the very articulation of the cause-and-effect sequence, and exposed the fallacy of its basic assumption—*post hoc propter hoc* (after this [therefore] because of this). Theologians were not wrong when they pointed to Hume as the great mischief-maker of modern times. In the degree to which they clung to Aristotelian vestiges of the cause-and-effect sequence in their accounts of God's agency, their own constructions *ipso facto* became invalidated, and the stage was set for what Andrew D. White would call in a famous title, "the warfare of science with theology in Christendom."[1]

But the theologians had not been the only ones to bear the brunt of the attack. The scientists themselves, where they still held on to methods now falling into disrepute, had by the same token lost contact with their advancing army. Soon Immanuel Kant, proceeding upon Hume's critique, would clear the status of both mathematicians and natural scientists willing to restrict their understanding to the categories and principles of phenomena within experience. In the next breath, so to speak, he would expose any attempt on the part of speculative metaphysicians to extend this same understanding in a transcendent manner beyond the bounds of sense experience, to mere "beings of thought" (*noumena*). To him such attempts could lead only to illusions concerning the soul, the world, and God.

It is incorrect to construe the Kantian critique as having sounded the death knell of all metaphysics. There remained ample room for the age-old discipline, provided its repentant representatives became willing to repair to the Canossa of legitimate scientific endeavor. Provided also they satisfied themselves with whatever knowledge may be inferred from the *a priori* form of what is in the world of phenomena on the one hand, or from the *a priori* form of obligation, of what ought to be in the realm of morals on the other. Heeding at all times a basic difference between the use of understanding in the realm of phenomena and that of reason in the realm of ideas, there remained precious possibilities of figuring out either a mental picture of what the universe is like for us, or even gaining access to a concept of the Supreme Being sufficiently determined, again for us. While any determination of what the soul, the universe, and the Supreme Being may be in themselves was out of the question, there remained the possibility of a kind of knowledge susceptible of orienting and directing both our intellectual and our moral life. In other words, informed and critical minds could yet gain access to a tenable rational faith. Kant insisted that he had actually marked out the limitations of legitimate knowledge in order to make room for a legitimate faith. To him, the pseudodogmatism of traditional metaphysics proved to be the source of all unbelief.

With special reference to the notion of causality, Kant made it clear that it merely referred to one of the ways in which reason, in the form of understanding, prescribes its laws to the world of sense experience. So-called causes and effects accordingly result when reason impresses the seal of its own structure upon data already molded by the human intuition of time and space. And so it is the perceiving and thinking subject who produces the phenomenon. It is our human make-up which in turn makes causes and effects, building them into an ordered cosmos. Hence, philosophers and scientists have been led further to discount even modernized versions of the cause-and-effect sequence or "reason" of happenings. One after another these versions have been exposed as mostly projections of our human structure and motivation into the economy of reality.

In quantum physics the classical notion of law has for a large part yielded to a statistical formulation, that is, one similar to the kind of mental picture which is obtained when authorities attempt to evaluate the number of fatalities likely to be recorded on the Labor Day weekend, or the number of cars likely to cross the Golden Gate Bridge on the Fourth of July. This, as we shall see in detail, is due to the fact that indeterminacy seems to be inherent in the microscopic realm. And so in the estimation of the originator of quantum physics himself, Max Planck, what once stood for causality has become mostly a heuristic principle, a fruitful way of asking questions as a child does.[2] In the same mood, one of the most eminent specialists of our day on causation, Léon Brunschvicg, has been satisfied to conclude a lifelong historical approach to the subject in its many ramifications,[3] with the terse pronouncement that to speak of causality at all amounts to saying that "there is a universe." These two testimonies truly exemplify the trend of scientific thinking in our time.

It may accordingly be asserted that reasoning by the cause, more especially in terms of the final cause or purpose supposed to be at work in the universe, has been eliminated by science. To think otherwise would seem to amount to wishful speculation on the part of a man unable to jump outside his own shadow.

What process of reasoning may then be said to have been substituted by the new science for the ancient way of reasoning by the cause? To the consideration of this all-important question we now turn.

3

The Way of Mental Construction

LONG forgotten are the days when Francis Bacon exposed Aristotelianism only to advocate a descriptive, qualitative, and classificatory method grounded in an empiricism which was much closer to Aristotle than to the scientific method well at work among his own contemporaries. The plain fact is that Bacon was at odds with the mathematical method which henceforth displaced the ancient empirical approach. He went as far as to blame Copernicus for having disregarded the real motions of earth and sun so long as his mathematical formulas checked with the observations.

The advent of modernity in the scientific realm actually was marked by the rejection of the old approach through the empirical data of consciousness, and the substitution for it of a series of intellectual constructions based on mathematics. The resulting depersonalization of the mental pictures obtained in the process has led critics to maintain that brilliancy of achievement has been realized at the cost of obscurity of understanding. The fact is that the very expediency which liberated science from empirical methods and thus allowed it to progress by leaps and bounds, especially in physics, has meant an increasing recourse to mathematical models fruitful in what Vaihinger has called "useful fiction." What modernity would seem to imply in the scientific realm is a rift between too anthropomorphic a concept of knowledge on the one hand, and purer mathematical forms of logic on the other.

Instead of venturing a debatable personal opinion on the subject and in order to avoid lengthy disquisitions, let me simply point to the most recent, most striking occasion when the rift now under scrutiny came to full expression. The confrontation of views took place between Albert Einstein and Viscount Herbert L. Samuel, president of the Royal Institute of Philosophy, at a meeting of the British Association for the Advancement of Science in Edinburgh, during the month of August, 1951.

The immediate occasion of the debate, however, was Lord Samuel's book, *Essays in Physics,* published earlier in the year.[1] In this book the author felt constrained to expose some of the "fateful" consequences of the new approach. Granting that this mathematical approach belonged in the special sciences where it had proved so fruitful, the author failed to see why it should have become so exclusive as to imply a surrender of the well-established empirical approach to reality through the data of sense experience and its deeper implications. As he saw it, it was as impossible for a mental picture like that of space to affect a process of nature, as it would be for a zoo to include in its collections a centaur or a sphinx. This failure to provide a causal explanation he even detected in Newton's law of inertia. The fact is that he looked at Newton in this connection very much as Bacon had looked at Copernicus. Newton stated that a body perseveres in a state of rest, or of uniform motion in a straight line, unless it is compelled to change that state by forces acting thereon; but, Lord Samuel insisted, he did not attempt to discuss the why or the how of this. Scientists not only fail to provide the answer to such questions, but it is customary for them nowadays not to attempt, nor even wish, to provide them. Further taking to task scientific treatises, Lord Samuel exposed their way of disguising as causes linguistic postulations like "conservation of momentum" or "properties of space" as though these actually were factual physical events.

Lord Samuel contended that only by maintaining side by side the two types of approach, i.e., the empirical and the mathematical, may we hope to safeguard the meaning of scientific research, as well as its significance for man. What was needed, then, was the rehabilitation side by side with the mathematical method of what had been known from time immemorial as explanation by the cause. By this he meant the establishment of an analogy between a new phenomenon and a *familiar* phenomenon, ultimately between scientific principles and a daily human experience drawing its notion of reality from the data of consciousness. To illustrate, "energy" may be regarded as the basic reality in nature because it actually is known to us from a daily experience which now includes that of an atomic explosion. The kind of "real explanation" Lord Samuel suggested, accordingly, could not be confined to a precise mathematical model but should prove satisfactory for analogy with our daily experience.

The depth and comprehensive character of Lord Samuel's argument, I submit, far transcends corresponding treatments in current literature on the subject, including religious literature. This is why evangelical Christians will always be amply rewarded for a reasonable amount of extracurricular reading. It is needless to insist that the statement just made applies *a fortiori* to an acquaintance with Einstein's evaluation of Lord Samuel's views.

Einstein made his answer in a most courteous letter, together with a 1,300-word enclosure in German, which Lord Samuel included in his book.[2] As Einstein saw it, Lord Samuel called for a science concerned with the description of what is "physically real." Hence any attempt on the part of physicists to manage with purely fictitious concepts like number, would prevent them from reaching

their goal. As if physics were based on concepts somewhat analogous to the "smile of the absent cat"! Einstein remarked jokingly.

Then came the thrust. In fact "the 'real' is in no way immediately given to us. Given to us are merely the data of our consciousness; and among these data only those form the material of science
which allow of univocal linguistic expression. There is only one
way from the data of consciousness to 'reality,' to wit, the way of
conscious or unconscious intellectual construction, which proceeds
completely free and arbitrarily."[3] Our starting point in everyday
thinking with reference to reality, Einstein further argued, is the
elementary concept of continually existing objects like the table in
my room. Yet, it is not the table as such which is given to me, but
a mere complex of sensations to which I ascribe the name and concept "table." And this is a speculative-constructive kind of approach based on intuition.

It is indeed of the greatest importance that we should be made
aware of the element of construction which is already implied at
this point, otherwise we easily should be "misled by the illusion
that the 'real' of our daily experience 'exists really' "[4] as our sense
experience conveys it to us. Conversely we should be tempted also
to treat the physicist's constructions as " 'mere ideas' separated
from the 'real' by an unbridgeable gulf."[5] The truth of the matter
is, however, that in physics the correspondence or correlation between our concepts and our sensations becomes all the more indirect as purer mathematical models are devised.

What then is our justification in elaborating such models? Essentially this, that our choice of the elements we apply in the construction of physical reality turns out to be successful. Increasingly,
therefore, we are putting more trust in our mental constructions
than in the everyday way of intuiting reality at the level of mere
consciousness. Whereupon followed in Einstein's enclosure a
searching presentation of the various ways in which science had

been led to vindicate its mathematical approach, from the classical physics of Newton to quantum and relativity through the work of men like Faraday and Maxwell.

The over-all impression left by the confrontation just concluded is that Lord Samuel found it hard to surrender the older empirical, anthropomorphic approach because it had become so familiar. Once more in his case familiarity had proved a stumbling block across the path of advance. It is noteworthy, for example, that the distinction Lord Samuel advocated between "quiescent energy" and "activated energy" with reference to the Newtonian principle of inertia, bore a striking resemblance to the account Aristotle gave of the phenomena involved. There is no doubt that Einstein's was the forward-looking view. Lord Samuel failed to take full cognizance of the paradox involved in the resulting tension. And this paradox may be stated as follows: as mathematical models to be applied to the physical world are perfected, and by the same token become all the more remote from the data of consciousness, this very remoteness allows a closer, more adequate evaluation of the same world. But what is this if not a new way of stating the perennial truth that the more I understand, the more I become able to penetrate reality; the higher the flight into the intelligible, the deeper the subsequent dent into the real? Thus the insistent suggestion forced upon us ever since our opening pages that an anthropomorphic empiricism may well lie at the root of our trouble, has now come to full expression in the light of the most perfected forms of knowledge available in our time.

This obviously should not be construed as implying that the mathematical method so successfully applied in the realm of physics is susceptible of being extended to other realms, or in any way generalized. Still less does it imply that physics has become synonymous with science in general—an illusion current in the public mind. The plain fact is that Aristotle, who was first and foremost a biologist, did not choose to make full use of his undeniable knowledge of mathematics probably because his interest in the phenomena of life required a method of analysis and organization not provided by mathematics. For none was in a better position than he was in his day, to evaluate rightly the possibilities of an approach so ably developed by the Babylonians, the Egyptians, and by mathematicians of the caliber of Pythagoras and Plato. What Aristotle realized as to the limitations of the mathematical approach to biology, Socrates had already discovered with respect to ethics. This awareness in fact happens to provide a perfect clue to the plot of any Socratic dialogue, as well as to the Socratic method of *reductio ad absurdum*. Socrates had detected an essential weakness in the application of geometrical models to the establishment of basic assumptions on ethical values. Accordingly he would assume one possibility without accepting it himself, and by means of successive attacks on alternatives force the proponents concerned to admit contradiction or even absurdity. At best he would lead them to confess that the issue could not be settled with any degree of finality.

Let me simply conclude on this point that those who would advocate an extension of the mathematical method so successfully applied in physics, to the biological and human sciences, had better rediscover the facts of life as they were known centuries before Christ. Adequate categories admittedly must be developed for the various realms of scientific activity, whether in the biological, the human, or the theological sciences, together with corresponding modifications of methodology.

The preceding concessions and assertions leave us all the more free to state that what has been said thus far adds up to an imperative *caveat* with regard to the radical anthropomorphism of an empirical method proceeding upon the mere data of consciousness. Techniques of construction based on Vaihinger's notion of useful fiction[6] are now being developed and generalized in widely different realms of investigation, as indeed they were meant to be by Vaihinger himself. These techniques are proving increasingly fruitful. It is regrettable, however, that the word "fiction" had to be used to characterize perfectly legitimate types of mental construction. I have seen Christian thinkers reject the very thought of useful fiction without a hearing merely because of the connotations suggested by its name. Sad to say, this is still the kind of mental attitude with which we have to cope at this late hour.

4

The Impact of Scientific Methods

WE ARE now in a position to understand better why even the most logical history of the "idea" of causality comes short of satisfactorily accounting for the drama of purpose. Such philosophical disquisition merely refers to surface phenomena. The real drama lies deeper. It is impervious to mere empirical interpretation. Always keeping in mind the reservations just made with reference to the advisability of generalizing or of simply extending to new realms the techniques of useful fiction, we would investigate further possibilities of mental construction in this matter of purpose; then we would probe deeper in order to check the resulting "models" against elemental reactions detected even beyond the organic. Ultimately we must reach for the religious motivation which proves primary. The drama of cosmic purpose in the last analysis *is* a religious drama. It is under this and related aspects that modernity will most likely be found to have affected its plot.

Life precedes knowledge. We act our knowledge before adequately formulated sets of assumptions more firmly direct our steps. The more adequate these formulations, the more likely they are to give the lie to the familiar interpretations we used to derive from the data of our consciousness. And so our thinking at its best has strange ways of resisting us. This is why it is at opposite poles from wishful thinking.

There is deep meaning in the ancient fable about a disheartened woodcutter who wearily dropped his load by the wayside and summoned Death. He made so little day in day out. And so many mouths to feed too! Then soldiers and tax-gatherers would pounce on him and exact a lion's share. What *was* the good of it all? Oh, that Death would only come! But then to his utter amazement Death did come.

"What do you want of me?" the Reaper asked in earnest.

"Oh . . . nothing! Nothing at all!" the man mumbled. Whereupon he added nervously, no doubt to appease the possibly irascible apparition, "Ah, yes. Kindly help me put back that load of wood on my shoulders."

Deep within him there ruled a primal will-to-live in spite of the most heart-rending woes which usually monopolized his thinking.

A strange echo of this same truth may be perceived once thought has been allowed full sway to complete its course. Thus after a laborious inquiry through the classics, music, philosophy and theology, New Testament scholarship, medicine, and Indian lore, Albert Schweitzer was forced back upon elemental thinking. The basic assumption suddenly forced upon him was, "I am life that wills-to-live in the midst of life that wills-to-live." Then "unforeseen and unsought" came the phrase, "Reverence for Life." Truly an unexpected encounter with purpose in its pristine freshness.

Deep-seated meanings of purpose come to light at this point. Thus psychologists of Freudian inspiration insist that no human action is without purpose, whether we laugh or dream or become victims of a slip of the tongue. The fact is that the muscles of the tongue released and immediately oriented by inner, often repressed drives, may prove more truthful than the tongue actually meant to be at the service of the prepared statement. The late president of Union Theological *Seminary* in New York was quick to realize this when, a man having asked him on the telephone whether this was "Union *Cemetery*," his retort swiftly came:

"Yes, and this is Dr. Coffin speaking."

Truly a case where, in the words of Sigmund Freud, "a preconscious train of thought is for a moment left to a process of unconscious elaboration, from which it emerges in the form of a witticism."[1]

A still more deep-seated view of purpose appears in the body's fight for survival as considered from the human standpoint in terms of the intended. This of course does not *ipso facto* imply that the purpose we read back into the process at hand actually constitutes a purpose in itself. Supposing, for instance, bacteria get into a wound. Phagocytes are attracted, possibly by some chemical stimulus, to the point of the bacterial invasion. Certain types of antibodies known as opsonins, which are specific for different diseases, enable the phagocytes to attack the bacteria by engulfing them. Thus an invading bacterium is likely to be crowded, then cornered by a jellylike substance. Next a hole is opened in the membrane which surrounds that substance in the manner of a skin, and the bacterium is eaten up and seemingly digested. No wonder finalistic interpretations easily suggest themselves to the candid observer.

The next step is to extend purpose further to the consideration of animal psychology, yet merely as a systematic description of sequences ending in the achievement of a goal, whether or not there is awareness of this on the part of the animal. The chance of error here once more is that of anthropomorphism on the part of the observer. Yet there can hardly be any question of anthropomorphism in the case of my dog scratching the door in order to get in!

And so it becomes clear that human notions of purpose actually belong in a still more widely extended view somehow pertaining to the deeper reality of the things that *are*. This is why our disheartened woodcutter did not quite understand what was happening to him. Neither did even the learned Albert Schweitzer. Yet we now come to see that these are not isolated cases. They rather prove to be illustrations of a basic human situation. Purpose is encountered sometimes before a man is enabled to define a purpose of his own. And when he does formulate a definition, he may do so only to be confronted by an entirely different one which turns out to be the real one. This kind of happening amid the pressing needs and demands of life strikes a man in terms of what Gabriel Marcel has called "exigency." The realities involved in accusation and guilt pertain to the same realm, as Nietzsche has pointed out. The regularity of certain events, still more that of chance occurrence or recurrence, sometimes seems to "cause" causality. Does not chance operate very much like an intention? To our contemporary primitives there is no doubt about this. As they see it, nothing whatsoever is what we call accidental—a curious version of pagan Calvinism. It is a fact that seen from the outside predestination and doom look much alike. Viewed from the inside they are of course at opposite poles. Predestination points to an all-knowing Providence. Doom is ascribed to baleful virtues or blind forms of fate best detected by divination or trial by ordeal.

At this point, let us probe deeper and reach for the "given" of a religious motivation likely to baffle our familiar ways of thinking.

Admittedly there was reality in Greek religion, in that its gods were conceived of as living beings lording it over the will of men. While each god had his own jurisdiction, Zeus, the god of the sky who ruled over heavenly phenomena, was king. But even he, like all the gods, was subject to the consent of Destiny which might be disclosed through his wife and sister Hera, the queen of the gods.

There resulted a willful pattern of fate and doom which could only in part be deciphered through the Delphic oracle of Apollo.

The Homeric notion of fate or necessity was conceived as an abstract power, *Moira* or *Aisa,* both words really meaning "apportionment." But then the *Moirai* later became spirits of birth. They were spinners generally thought to be old women, three in number, and were often identified as *Klotho* (spinner), *Lachesis* (she of the lot), and *Atropos* (inflexible). The primary fact still remains that the goddess of fate, *Moira,* was regarded as assigning to everyone his portion of good or evil although he may increase evil, nay, play into the hands of fate, by his own folly. This squares perfectly with the notion of the tragic flaw as characterized in the thirteenth section of Aristotle's *Poetics,* with reference to the nature of the tragic hero. Similarly the Latin *Fatum,* which presumably referred to the "spoken" decree of the gods, like *Moira* was occasionally used in the plural, *Fata,* and pointed to these same spinners. *Fatum, Fata* then became *fae,* our English fairy (in French *fée*), just as *pratum, prata* became our English prairie (in French, *pré, prairie*). Finally the Greek *Moira* in the meaning of "apportionment" or *pars,* gave *Parca, Parcae,* the Fates (French *Parques*), designating these same spirits which lorded it over birth and the "apportionment" made at the time of birth. Yet all of this notwithstanding, both *Moira* and *Aisa* were sometimes identified with Zeus, just as they occasionally were differentiated from him as superseding him.

The force implied in necessity was encountered immediately in natural wants like thirst and hunger and in sufferings like bodily pain. These encounters were at the root of *anagke*—Latin, *necessitas.* There truly was something fatal about them; yet the resulting urge could be circumvented by proper dispositions, at least to a certain degree. The most impressive encounter of man, his encounter with death, could not be circumvented thus. It was only later that death was integrated into the cosmological concept of order as it developed through the idealization of law or "fixed measure," *dike*. I say "idealization" because the original sense was the empirical induction derived from custom, usage, manner, as in the sentence, "This is the manner of old men." And just as the Ionians sought to find out what was the manner of an orderly *cosmos,* Solon and Clisthenes sought to formulate what was the manner of an orderly *polis.* In this and similar ways the endeavor to bring cosmos out of chaos became the ideal of Greek metaphysics and science.

At the root of this ideal we find a concern which goes through law and necessity back to a will. In *Oedipus King of Thebes,* singled out by Aristotle as a most representative and perfect drama, Jocasta thinks that Apollo can be cheated of his will; but her wishful thinking is in vain. Weaving the very warp and woof of a pattern of power, the Immortals—they had no blood—held the answers to the deeper "why" of life. All the time we know that Jocasta is to die someday because she is a human being, but in all evidence we are faced with the deeper issue as to *why* Jocasta should die in the midst of such horrible circumstances. Behind the fact that she was to die someday there was a law. Behind the fact that she should die in such tragic circumstances there was a will. While it is true, then, that this uncanny will superseded the gods at least in part, the gods were the instruments, the *media* of that will, and in more than one way its incarnation. This being granted in the main, we must admit that the collective notions involved are often far from clear to Aristotelian ways of thinking. A consideration of the folklore of our Western world confirms this impression while bearing witness to similar views.

According to the tradition of the Middle Ages, the fairies were present the night Ogier the Dane was born, each to bestow upon

him a different gift. The belief in fairies is still alive in some parts
of Europe. The peasants in those districts know that the fairies
come down the chimneys into their houses to care for the children,
whose future they foretell. The fairies in Brittany, the Korrigans,
not only know the future; they even direct the forces of nature and
can change into any form that pleases them. This is likewise one
of the great prerogatives of witches. Like them also the fairies can
transport themselves from one end of the world to the other in
the twinkle of an eye. Each year the Korrigans celebrate the return
of spring by a nocturnal festival. After a mysterious moonlight
feast they vanish with the dawn. According to the folklore of
Brittany these Korrigans are supposed to be noble Gallic princesses
whom God cursed for not having accepted Christianity when the
apostles came. They are moved by a mortal hatred for the clergy
and the Virgin. If Saturday is an inauspicious day for fairies it is
because it is consecrated to Mary.

The fairies' wrath was feared for a long time. The folklore of
Ireland and Brittany testifies, for instance, to the practice of serv-
ing a feast to the fairies in a room adjoining that of a woman in
childbirth. So deeply rooted was the belief in fairies that every
year, even as late as the sixteenth century, a mass was celebrated
in certain churches to preserve the surrounding country against
evil fairies. As dethroned pagan divinities, adversaries of Christianity, and declared enemies of the clergy and the Virgin, the
fairies have long been exorcised. The grace with which they are
adorned is largely due to the poetic pattern of the tales. The plain
fact is that ancient collective notions of doom have deeply in-
filtrated the Western world, finding on all sides the support of
germane popular beliefs developed on the fringe of Christian
views.

Further insight into this complex pattern of doom is provided
in a drama which may be unique in this connection, because it also

affords the opportunity of observing the ancient pagan fate in a Christian atmosphere. I mean, of course, *Macbeth*. In the weird sisters, Shakespeare introduced a notion of fate still very much alive in the Scandinavian folklore. Their very name, as borrowed from the second edition of Raphael Holinshed's *Chronicle* (1587), actually came from the Anglo-Saxon *wyrd*, meaning "fate." It was only for the sake of the problem of communication that Shakespeare presented these "goddesses of destiny" under the guise of familiar witches killing swine and brewing hell-broth. Of course Shakespeare never intended to formulate a theological problem. He was satisfied with the powerful suggestion of a human situation dominated and ruled by a mysterious will made far more intelligible in the Christian context of his day and age. And so, instead of the sacred horror of Sophocles in the face of an obscure destiny, we have a striking illustration of the biblical truth of death being the wages of sin.

Now one of the ways by which modern science has overcome doom—and this essentially by implication—is by substituting ever more adequate sets of assumptions for the weird constructions placed by former generations upon their encounters with events. Conversely there is no doubt that the mental pictures involved have become more and more remote from the pattern so familiar on the old empirical, anthropocentric level. For, may I ask, what remains of this familiar pattern in the statement that the probability that two independent events will happen simultaneously or in succession is the product of the probability of the two events taken singly? But who would contest that this very remoteness also allows a closer, truer evaluation of a situation brought about by a primitive encounter with chance happenings?

I refer to the formulation of the laws of chance and to the rise of the theory of probability. The calculus of probabilities would aim at reducing to numbers, as far as feasible, both the perplexing aspects of the universe about us and the uncertainties of life. Before the reader dismisses as nonsensical the last part of this statement, he had better make sure that he owns no insurance policy, that he never tries to set a fair price in business transactions, that he is not the least interested in the economic behavior of his country, nor in the forecast of events likely to proceed from any particular specified cause, and not even concerned with the reliability of testimony. But I should rather interrupt what would prove too lengthy an enumeration. Have not the references already given implied at the outset the elimination of every one of us?

At this point, however, we must watch out for an important turn of events. While it is true to say that probability has risen up on the ruins of pagan doom, it must be conceded that probability conversely has brought about on the part of the scientists a reluctance to claim any meaning-reference whatsoever to reality. The ground for this seemingly bold statement lies in the very adequacy of probability as a category for a fruitful approach to small-scale phenomena. Now these are the phenomena ultimately reached by the physicist in his quest for an understanding of nature. As things have turned out, the realm of microphysics has been characterized by Heisenberg as ruled by a radical indeterminacy. Whenever the quantum physicist attempts to penetrate the microcosm, he is confronted by an area of analysis in which the words "position" and "velocity" no longer may be used with accuracy beyond specified limits. A rigorous determinism no longer can be ascribed to the behavior of phenomena, such as used to rest on the possibility of determining simultaneously the initial position and velocity of a particle. Accordingly, the laws under consideration can be only the laws of probability, and this is why probability proves so adequate a category for the physicist. I have already pointed out that these same laws prove to be mere statistical laws. As such they tell us no more about a real nature than do casualty statistics about the identity of those who are to die over the Labor Day weekend. We should, however, not presume on what the future may or may not have to say on this admittedly thorny subject, as the Bohr principle of complementarity suggests. Though the quantum theory is indeterministic in its formulation, it may not by the same token be pronounced acausal in its reference to reality.

This in the main is the state of affairs which in part originated, and in part later vindicated, the scientific views which constitute the background of Bertrand Russell's *A Free Man's Worship,* to which an early allusion has been made.[3] In *Principia Mathematica,* mathematics has been derived from logic, both being finally fused into one single grammar of purely analytical concepts. The new discipline's essential aim, in other words, is to define mere validity with reference to axioms. It has been disentangled from whatever its original scientific scaffolding may have been. Under this purified form it constitutes a masterly introduction to a symbolic logic satisfied with providing any scientific activity with adequate means of integration. To ask the Bertrand Russell of the *Principia* to argue for the existence of God or posit the assumption of a cosmic purpose is to ask him to provide the very things he never meant to provide in the first place. I agree that when he steps out of this his special field to brag about not being a Christian, or establish "a hilarious catalogue of organized and individual stupidity" under the title head *An Outline of Intellectual Rubbish,* then the question is different. Yet it concerns first and foremost an individual who has mistaken logico-mathematical propositions for statements of fact about reality, in other words done the very thing the *Principia* cautions against. And this applies *a fortiori* to the pessimistic and gratuitous inference of Professor Stace also alluded to in our first chapter. Indeed, this kind of modernity may not be said to have killed religion but merely to have passed it by.

The main achievement of the *Principia,* as far as our inquiry is concerned, is on the one hand to have cleansed scholarly pursuits from the dross of empirical anthropomorphism, and on the other to have provided them with more adequate means of mental construction. On both counts the way to a basic certification of the human mind has been further cleared. For these reasons, therefore, we identify in the rise of both probability and symbolic logic, pointers and moves in the right direction—wishful thinking and deep-seated former prejudices to the contrary notwithstanding.

5

A Matter of Proper Jurisdiction

WHEN symbolic logic is used to figure out a mental picture of
the space-time world, the immediate outcome is a cold, mute, and
colorless picture. All data of sense experience are missing in such
a world model for the simple reason that personality has been removed from it. Thus the sensation of color becomes in the model
of the physicist an "objective" picture of waves, or showers of
photons, which does not begin to account for the sensation itself.
It also happens that when certain kinds of vibrations hit the retina
of a healthy eye, the person involved "sees" such or such a color.
The color itself has otherwise nothing in common with the electro-
magnetic phenomena which bring it about.

This means that no personality can ever become a part of the
scientist's world model. Neither can a personal God. That which
seems to have made the world picture accessible has accordingly
implied the removal from it of anything either personal or divine,
which accounts for the trivial remark that no scientist has ever
been able to find God anywhere, not even in the created world.
Strictly speaking, science cannot help but be atheistic. Neither
can it escape being characterized as "de-personalized activity,"
within the structure of a personality-producing universe.

The basic reason for the paradox is not far to seek. It lies in the incontrovertible fact that the world picture and the personality that constructs the picture are identical. Seen in terms of objectivation, this selfsame datum appears as a mental picture. Becoming self-conscious, it yields the immediate intuition of a personality which, as I believe, lives, moves, and has its being in the living God. Indeed the scientist who fails to find God in the space-time picture may be likened to that middle-class fellow who had been speaking prose for forty years without ever having become aware of the fact. Molière's famous character had been born of the ego idea when he said, "I am a man of noble birth." He had, as it were, superimposed this ego idea upon the phenomenal man he saw when looking at himself in the mirror. Such superimposition is the sort of thing we all indulge in early in life. It is in fact the first important step we take, not only with reference to ourselves, but by the same token with reference to our fellow men.

We begin by identifying the ego idea with our body, together with its sentient, percipient, and thinking equipment. We say, "I am healthy;" "She is putting on weight;" "He is worth one hundred thousand dollars." Whereupon, superimposition follows upon superimposition: "We won the game;" "They elected a President." Ultimately, the ego idea is extended to the point of identification with our world view. Thus Pascal in a famous passage: "Let man . . . consider what he is compared with the reality of things; regard himself lost in this remote corner of nature; and from the tiny cell where he lodges, to wit the universe, weigh at true worth earth, kingdoms, towns, himself. What is man face to face with infinity?"[1]

The fact is that the immediately given is a loose canvas of consciousness into which are woven the experiences, images, and memories which progressively make up our world picture. The mental models of the scientist also belong in this context, inasmuch as they are constructs elaborated upon that base. This remains true even when the outreach of the mind is greatly increased by means of mechanical devices and recording sets such as the electron microscope or the Schmidt camera. For all of these are man-made, and the data they yield, man-interpreted. They would otherwise be of no use.

Now to all practical purposes the immediate implication of the activities involved is to bring about an artificial dichotomy between subject and object. Henceforth a distinction is made between the immediate data of consciousness and the intelligible picture the mind elaborates in order to explain such data. The dimensions of personality originally are found to be not only biographical and social, but man may be said to "think" with his whole body, the same organism being one with what will later be apprehended as its "environment." We make our panorama of the setting in which we live into a mirror and a reflection of ourselves. Thus we find the "inner" self not only reflected in the "outer" world, but coloring it and colored by it. Such vital symbolism is basic to our make-up. It becomes basic to our world view.

In a real way, our pristine human situation is that of a human being belonging to a world of nature to which he looks with hope or dread, for benevolent or hostile intervention. Our first notions with regard to this nature may hardly be said at this stage to be founded upon knowledge. Activity, feelings, sensations—extremely rich ones—contribute to these notions. Yet this original endowment remains mostly unanalyzed. Its total impact is an immediate, intense experience. Not only are such undifferentiated elements represented in a number of ways; they are felt and acted simultaneously because rich in motivating power. This is the reason why an individual may be so deeply affected when his name is mentioned. His self-assertion amounts to an emergence from a network of "participations," of "appurtenances" experienced within a welter of deep, expanding life. The upshot of it all is a type of mind which has not yet disentangled itself from the luxuriance of myth and symbol.

Objectivation in its first steps amounts to a progressive breaking apart from surroundings into which one had remained absorbed. It is a slow awakening analogous to that of Mallarmé's Faun in his poem "The Afternoon of a Faun," in which the creature struggles hard to dispel a clinging world of dream, moving his legs, shaking his curved horns from the entwining vegetation, struggling to emerge from that "mass of ancient night" which thus far has obscured his soul. As existential forms of thought dimly seek to assert themselves, vital symbols lose their luxuriant coloring; they shrink under the pressure of classification and definition. They are on their way to becoming objective signs, truly inanimate pictures and mental models. The symbol is lost in the objective mental picture as thought is depersonalized by socialization. Hence so many tragic moments, crises of childhood uprooted into adolescence, then into intellectual maturity.

Our scientific culture considers depersonalized and widely socialized abstractions to be the supreme good which conditions all other forms of goodness, and especially the general direction of life. This implies a departure from the real, that is, from the *res,* from the data of experience. Each departure may be seen as a separate act whose avowed purpose is a quest for more permanent patterns of clues, notions which precede and outlive the particular cases which "prove" them—in other words, mental pictures independent of the specific instances in which they are actualized. Such models represent all sorts of possibilities and allow man to organize his world with a view to useful application of his newly acquired knowledge. By reason of the type of existence suggested by our so-called "laws of nature," the intelligible comes to govern the changing mobility of the real.

We may henceforth consider the modern scientist as one who

long since proceeded from the sensibly real to speculate on the intelligible so that he might formulate clever patterns of clues likely to fit selected groups of facts to the satisfaction of an enlightened majority. This is what he calls truth, and he rightly omits both the definite article and the capital T. Thus I recently heard Dr. J. Robert Oppenheimer state in answer to a question on this specific point, "I do not use the notion." Whereupon, an inquirer having pressed the case with reference to God, the director of the Institute for Advanced Study merely dropped the remark, "I do not use the term. I find it ambiguous." To one who had made himself at home in the intelligible realm of mental pictures, God had indeed become a mere "term," and an ambiguous one at that. While an exclusive preoccupation with the realm of mental models allows the scientist an ever steadier mastery over nature in terms of H-bombs and moon satellites, it ultimately may shape his whole being and outlook for better or for worse.

The process of objectivation implies in human nature a progressive dichotomy likely to issue in estrangement from a man's original endowment. This may turn out to be a serious situation. Let our scientist recover his humanity simply by being involved in an automobile accident, for example, and he may soon find out for himself. It is not only that his detached speculation and occasional findings may well have little to do with the deeper reality of the things that are. Truth worthy of the name is ultimately simple. In the situation at hand, the making of mental pictures implies an eclipse of personality, and this essentially because the thinking person and his world pictures are one and the same datum. It is high time for those who understand the splitting of the atom to realize the elemental fact of the disruption involved in the process of objective thinking and "picture-making." For this disruption involves the loss of the original rich primitive endowment of consciousness, of which personality is the core—personality in man, personality in God.

In the context of objectivation, the counterpart of the scientist may be found in the poet who inclines more especially toward a rich primitive experience. That is why we admire the luxuriance and suggestive power of his poems which are attempts at emulating the Creator. I have no great belief in intellectual poetry, although it seems to be the fashion in certain contemporary circles, because abstraction implies extraction, that is, impoverishment. The richest forms of expression are those of symbol and myth which catch the most elusive aspects of experience alive as it were and let them live, while cold abstraction actually comes to rest in artifice, immobility, and death.

Objectivation is the price we must pay for thinking at all, a price which can be safely agreed to only by those who remain constantly aware of the conditions implied in the transaction. This statement applies both to those who choose to live empirically at the level of experience, and those who elect to speculate in the realm of the intelligible. Nothing has been said in the preceding pages that may be construed as detracting one iota from Einstein's answer to Lord Samuel, as analyzed at length in a previous chapter. The scientific way remains that of mental construction, and the elaboration of mental pictures or models does reach to perfection once reduced to mathematical terms. Lord Samuel, on the other hand, has provided us with a good illustration of a scientist unwilling to pay the full price for his flight into the rarefied atmosphere of symbolic logic. To put the matter in common speech, he wanted to eat his cake and have it too.

A great many misunderstandings arise from such doublemindedness, more especially in the religious realm. Men of God crave the certification of the human mind. In this laudable mood certain of them claim to have bridged the gap between "reason" and "faith" in terms acceptable to the scientist. In so doing, theologians who want to safeguard at all cost the scientific character of their undertaking unconsciously allow their disquisitions to turn into some form of apologetics. It will readily appear in these pages, I hope, that the certification of the human mind, however desirable it may be, is both conditioned and limited. Enough has already been said to account for this situation.

The life of faith remains at all times close to the shores of experience. Theological understanding deals with intelligible mental constructs meant to secure some measure of comprehension, once they are "brought down" from the realm of abstraction to come to grips with experience. Freely granting the fact that these two ways of approach to the same basic reality pertain to the unity of human nature, and accordingly crave the certification of the human mind, they nevertheless must be acknowledged as two independent ways of approach. This may be one of the reasons why there are more theologians than holy men under the blinding sun of the Gospel. If a way to wholeness is to be found, it must be that of elemental thinking out of respective bases, each of them clearly defined and strongly held. Albert Schweitzer independently came close to this view when he wrote:

Spiritual truth is concerned with the knowledge of what we must become spiritually in order to be in a right relationship to God. It is complete in itself. It is intuitive knowledge of what ought to be in the realm of the spirit. All other knowledge is of a different kind, having to do, not with what happens in us, but what goes on in the world—a field in which understanding can only be limited and liable to change.[2]

In accordance with this conclusion I shall continue in the following chapters to write in terms of the subject-object dialectical tension, since this is the price we must all pay for the privilege of thinking. In so doing, however, I shall at all times remain aware of the artifice involved in the fact of objectivation which conditions my thinking. Let me simply say, then, that using the current grammar of concepts will constitute one of the ways of paying tribute to useful fiction.

The dialectical tension to keep in mind if we are to avoid confusion amounts to a distinction between biblical experience and theological understanding.

PART II

The Biblical Experience
and Theological Understanding

6

Preliminary Words of Caution

As WE are about to consider the record of biblical experience, we need to be made aware of an insidious tendency likely to lead us astray at the outset. I refer to the mind's natural, mostly unconscious propensity to familiar, anthropomorphic views. If not carefully heeded, this mental predisposition may result in a radical distortion of the perspective at hand. It shows up in every realm of human life, even in the most trivial occurrences.*

The familiar setting constitutes for us the substantial reality to which we revert as through a law of our being. The substantial character of the experience is happily suggested in Coleridge's phrase, "palpable and familiar." And just as we are at home in the familiar, so are we likely to be homesick in strange surroundings. The experience recalled by George Pope Morris speaks to the condition of many of us:

> In other countries, when I heard
> The language of my own,
> How fondly each natural word
> Awoke an answering tone.[1]

* The substance of what follows in this chapter has already been made the object of my editorial for *Theology Today,* v. 15, 1 (April 1958), 1–8, yet was originally part of the manuscript of the present book.

Natural words act upon us as do familiar names. Once more it took a poet to apprehend this deep affinity. Thus Shakespeare exalted the magic of names as familiar in one's mouth "as household words." The familiar gives us a sense of security in the midst of precarious circumstances, that is, of circumstances that call for prayer. And so to revert to the safe haven of the familiar often turns out to be for us a mostly unconscious way of praying.

Where our treasure is, there will our heart be also. Because he so highly values the pearl of great price, the Christian is likely to experience more deeply than others this gravitation of the mind back to the familiar.

There is something sacred about the familiar. This word "sacred" originally meant untouchable, as in the Latin dictum, *Res est sacra miser* (the miserable one is untouchable), where a primitive connotation is readily apprehended. The perennial character of such primitive views must be ascribed to a deep-seated misoneism, or fear of innovation. As primitives see it, to innovate is to expose oneself to the most dreadful dangers. A pertinent motto for the primitive landscape of reality could read, "Do not disturb."

As subsequent meanings of the word "sacred" come to light, it appears that the sacred object is no longer only the untouchable object, but further the desired, beloved object. In this connection our young people today may find it worthwhile to dwell on the tradition of courtly love as it developed through the twelfth and thirteenth centuries. I refer especially to the devotion of the Knights of the Round Table to their lady in that state of near-worship which was then coming to fuller expression in the Virgin cult. It is historically true to say that the highest expression of human love originated in religious mysticism. And so as we speak of the sacredness of the familiar, we find ourselves treading on holy ground.

The reason I have insisted on this question of origin is that it helps us understand why we should respect views of long standing. They constitute patterns of sacred memories through which the soul perseveres in a wisdom unaware of itself. That wisdom we call tradition. It should never be lightly tampered with, still less allowed to become an object of ridicule. What may mislead many of us is that the deeper the roots, the better hidden they are. Conversely, the familiar becomes all the more sacred as its origins are lost in the night of ancient days. Hence the impression on the part of the faithful that things have always been as they are now found to be. The *status quo* accordingly may be felt to pertain to the very order of God. No wonder a religious fear is likely to be aroused at the thought that it might ever be disturbed.

One of the reasons some people are so hard on Fundamentalism is that they are so ignorant of the distant origins of that position. Casting ridicule upon it is the natural reaction of detractors whose memory hardly goes further back than the year of our Lord 1909 when millions of copies of *The Fundamentals* published in Los Angeles spread over the Protestant world, preparing the way for the Christian Fundamentals League and the World's Christian Fundamental Association. Henceforth slogans take over, and the whole conservative position is easily dismissed amid catcalls and name-calling. The very name Fundamentalist is even currently abbreviated for the sake of brevity in final judgment. Whereupon the straw man supposed to incarnate the backward beliefs freely ascribed to him is summarily disposed of. It is nevertheless a fact that he may have been an earnest Christian, as has often proved to be the case.

The plain truth is that the Fundamentalist attitude constitutes by birth and by right one of the essential aspects of the Reformation. Men like Luther, and more especially the Renaissance scholar Calvin, blazed the trail in more than one way to the modern attitude toward the Bible. What actually happened is that having opened the Scriptures to the laity, the Reformers were led by controversy to claim indiscriminately for the whole Bible an absolute authority thenceforth substituted for that of the Church of Rome. Their theological interpretations of the Book moreover remained controlled by the traditional *schema*. The main point is that the Fundamentalist's affirmation of the infallibility of Scripture originally was that of the Reformers. Were it only for this consideration, it should not be scornfully disparaged.

Sheer intellectual honesty would have us make a further acknowledgment with regard to this matter. As the Reformers opened the Book to the laity, an enthusiastic fervor greeted a Gospel now accessible in one's native tongue. Thus the Christian message was apprehended afresh in its pristine dynamism. A newness of life animated the Body of Christ. And further, there comes to light at this point another striking similitude between Fundamentalism and the Reformation. Making full allowance for occasional cases of smug complacency and lack of charity on the part of some Fundamentalists, an uncontrovertible belief in the verbal inspiration of all Scripture also generates today among the proponents of the ancient view the same enthusiastic fervor as of old. While many a sophisticated Christian feeds on an ersatz diet of learned up-to-date disquisitions, Fundamentalists are out in every sort of weather ringing doorbells. It is also a fact that Pentecostal sects hold the field in South America as well as on other continents where missionaries are at work. If it still be true that "by their fruit ye shall know them," what is to be the stand of many of us on the Day of Judgment?

Having thus attempted to do justice to Fundamentalism in the light of I Cor. 13, we must admit in the next breath that ignoring to all practical purposes a change of perspective wrought out over four centuries of cultural advances amounts to a serious declension.

It is a terrible thing for Christianity to allow itself to get out of touch with the world of men and affairs which is its mission field. I recently directed a university retreat in the "Bible Belt." There I found myself confronted by a generation of students who had been "conditioned" against the evangelical message. A discreet inquiry revealed that in practically every case they had been submitted to obsolete pressure methods of approach. It further appeared that quite a number of the younger instructors had already known a similar revulsion and, as a result, turned to Unitarianism. Moreover, currently available books had hardly proved a help. What purpose is ever served, may I ask, by reprint editions of obsolete theological dissertations, whose essential merit today is that they act as tranquilizers for cases of religious misoneism? What this means is that the vacuum, which has naturally appeared during the last fifty or sixty years in the production of ultraconservative biblical literature, is being artificially filled. Conversely, as new manuscripts catering to the old stereotyped outlook may not get access to the wider cultural market, they worm their way into that late nineteenth-century vintage of publications. The cultivation of obsolescence in this age of intense scientific progress truly has become an end in itself in a whole area of traditionalism.

Henceforth references to evangelism easily may be construed as labels of doubtful intellectual quality, and this is particularly grave in the midst of a generation groping for trustworthy guidance. We are undeniably confronted at this point with baleful aftereffects of the mind's gravitation back to the familiar.

Let us now turn to a somewhat composite group of conservatives, quite a number of whom have achieved distinction in their own special field. Anxious to steer clear of identification with Fundamentalism, they nevertheless remain equally concerned with an unswerving commitment to stereotyped views.

Their real intention is hardly veiled by seeming concessions made in the hope that the day may be at hand when the classical solution will once more come into its own. For this real intention is to all practical purposes conditioned by the mind's gravitation back to the familiar; in this case, back to the crystallized formulations of old. A man of goodwill may suggest that specific instances where havoc has been wrought by reactionary attitudes need not be duplicated. They may temporarily agree. Yet their next move may well be to call him in for the sake of slightly "emending" his wording. And this done, it would readily appear that the mind's gravitation back to the familiar had run its natural course.

This is not meant to imply that our neo-traditionalists agree among themselves. They do not. Just as the most bitter disagreements are likely to materialize between neighbors across the fence, so the sharpest theological arguments originate among those conservatives who differ on minor points. Give them a rank atheist, and they will love him because he is "convertible." It is the minor dissident that arouses their ire. Meanwhile the children of this world pass by the island of discord, as an army would disregard stragglers on the path of advance.

To ignore obvious difficulties is no way to dispose of them. Throw a problem out through the door, and it will reappear at the window. It is in many respects commendable to proclaim to a large gathering, "The Bible says . . . and the Bible says . . ." as if nothing of importance had ever happened since the later days of the Reformation to affect the total picture. Yet the receptive listener who steps forward is likely to find out for himself sooner or later that even the India paper which bears the sacred text is no longer negotiable at face value. Not that the text itself has lost any of its significance. Quite the contrary. It commands higher value than ever before, and this to the last word. It is merely that it has been identified as a dated and culturally conditioned human record of God's disclosure. Any profession of faith and statement of beliefs accordingly must proceed from both the account of events and the meaning actually implied in them in a given social and cultural context. Any attempt to perpetuate the element of relativity which may have become involved in the process is bound to bring the one who makes it out-of-touch with the later age in which he lives, and moves, and has his being. Not only does such a situation prevent useful communication with contemporaries, but it interferes with the knowledge of God and of his design.

The mind's gravitation back to the familiar has this in common with the larger aspect of gravitation: to ignore or hide its existence does not prevent its being there.

Our inquiry further brings us into contact with a rather likable group of Christians, conciliatory and ever ready to placate and mollify, yet withal anxious to hold on to the alloy of set ways of thinking. They are aware that the world in which they live keeps moving and that there can be no turning back of the clock. While accepting as inevitable the inroads of the well-established historical method into traditional interpretations, however, they are far from being wholehearted in their acceptance. In actual practice they welcome contributions likely to prove harmless while easing undeniable tensions. Yet they hardly control their wistful eagerness to have enough left of the old interpretations to carry on as usual. This is their way of not offending the congregation if they are in the ministry, or of professing Christianity with a tenable open-mindedness if they are in the pew. In the course of conversations with inquirers, they proceed in the same spirit, ready to concede the seemingly unessential. But then where is their frame of reference for essentiality? And so they essay a tentative give-and-take while holding on to what they cannot do without. In other words, they do their best to safeguard selected parts of their disintegrating profession, even while the facts which inspired it have been put in jeopardy. Their Christian conversation admittedly

[67]

may be admirable in actual practice, as if they wanted to atone for the confusion of their ideas.

Eclecticism has often sought in activity, if not in activism, ways of creating unity among discordant intellectual views. This tendency is well known in schools of philosophy. It is also noticeable in ecumenical gatherings where participants of different theological persuasions come to realize that they can work together even in the face of unresolved tensions in matters of doctrine. Yet in a case where all such tensions come to light within the same individual, it becomes obvious that a divided soul can hardly achieve that single-mindedness which makes light of obstacles encountered along the appointed way. Apart from a consistency grounded in a well-ascertained motivation, life is bound to be a succession of semantic nightmares in anguish and endless misery.

The mind's gravitation back to the familiar can never safely be taken for granted as a force in a component of forces. It must be squarely faced as a major source of disturbance across the path to maturity.

New Christian currency has been issued in the world of thought since the days of the Reformation. It does indeed bear the same old symbols. More surprising still, these symbols would seem to command higher value today than they ever did, were it only because the realities to which they point now may be ascertained with more accuracy. This is new currency nevertheless, a currency devised to meet the changing needs of a new social and cultural environment which implies new ways of thinking. The mind's gravitation back to the familiar notwithstanding, as adults we must face the fact that it is not what we like to hear, read, or see that constitutes the criterion of correctness, but the adequacy of our apprehension of the meaning and purpose of him who speaks to us. What matters in interpreting the Bible in particular is to apprehend and convey as accurately as possible the thought and intention of the original writer in his own situation.

Conservative Christians are right in insisting upon the wholeness of the Bible and in holding on to every word of the precious record. The fact of the matter is that the historical method of studying the Bible is equally insistent that it cannot possibly destroy a single word in that record. Its main concern is to find out what the words meant to say in the mind of those who used them. Once viewed in this light, the New Testament in particular bears witness to the faith of the early Christian community. To construe it otherwise amounts to distorting it. To set it within the living environment of the apostolic age that produced it safeguards its genuine meaning for all times, including our own.

There always will be those who will ascribe to God the kind of thinking they would do, were they in his place. Ours is happily a simpler task—namely, to figure out what God who meets us in and through the Bible actually says to us and expects from us. This we may safely do only as we counteract that ingrained tendency to gravitate back to the familiar.

7

A Record Contrary to Expectation

THE reason I have felt the need to emphasize the insidious dangers inherent in the mind's gravitation back to the familiar is that they constantly lurk along the path of our Reformed tradition. While tribute is due to the Reformers for having opened up the Bible to a large part of Christendom, the implication that the good Book could safely be read as it stood, without competent guidance and special preparation, gave free rein to the most undisciplined forms of individual interpretation. The Name of the Holy Spirit "speaking in the Scripture" was too often taken in vain. A satirical epigram had it that the Bible was the book where everyone could seek his own opinion with the assurance that he would find what he sought.

Once the biblical record is allowed to speak for itself, to provide its own answers to its own questions and according to its own categories of apprehension, the adequate perspective comes within view.

Perhaps the most striking feature in that restored perspective is that God is disclosed therein as the great Doer of the unexpected. This truly bewildering character comes to full expression in the "scandal of particularity" which, from the very core of Scripture, stares us in the face. It actually constitutes the significance of the

Bible—namely, that God's revelation has been given in historical events concerning a chosen people. Consider, on the one hand, the holy, all-wise, all-powerful nature of God; and on the other, the stubborn, crafty, and even treacherous character of Israel, together with its social and political insignificance. And yet the choice, however incredible, comes to pass with the call of Abraham.

The dimension of the unexpected overlays even the scandal of particularity. The very ways of God disclose it at every turn of events. Consider, for example, the mighty act through which a mass of depressed serfs are delivered from their Egyptian servitude in the midst of truly epic events. Again, think of the unexpected appearance of the sea-roving Philistines threatening the confederation of the clans of Israel, or of the sordid spectacle of the foolish and even criminal Israelites under Jeroboam II. Or pause to understand why God should have troubled to send Amos to those adulterous deniers of all justice in the midst of their fraud and perjury. To turn to yet another aspect of the "unexpected," why should such a man as Hosea have had to cope with an unfaithful wife, or a John the Baptist have fallen victim to the sadism of Herod? If God is the Almighty, how may we account for the fact that Jeremiah's exultant joy at Josiah's reform should so soon have turned to gloom, as the shrines and idols of yesterday seemed to have been removed only to make room for Temple worship and the trappings of its ritual? Why should Cyrus have been the instrument of the exiles' mighty deliverance from Babylon? And subsequently, how may one explain the utter lack of compassion shown by Israel in the face of pagan darkness, as exemplified in the Book of Jonah?

The New Testament bears further witness to the unexpected character of God's ways. I have already called to mind the dreadful fate of a seemingly forsaken John the Baptist. Does it not prove to have been a ghastly prelude to the cry of dereliction of Jesus on the Cross? What particularly draws attention, however, is the unexpected nature of the manner in which God wrought out his Purpose in the ministry of the man Christ Jesus. People came to him to see a wonder-worker. They were actually confronted by God's will for them. The ecclesiastics of the time might have been expected to do their utmost to help Jesus. Yet the most violent opposition he encountered came from them so that they were singled out by him for utter condemnation. Or think of the unexpected as a dimension of the disciples' experience. Their anticipation of the glory at hand came to naught on Calvary. They were left in utter dejection. And yet in the power of God their fellowship with the Lord was restored to them a hundredfold in the glow of Easter morning. Thereafter, his disciples were in closer fellowship with the living and abiding Christ, than the first disciples had ever been in the days of his flesh. Another extraordinary turn of history transformed Saul, the ruthless prosecutor of the Gentiles, into Paul, the greatest missionary the Christian cause has ever hailed. In vain had the high priest and Pilate, his accomplice, tried to annihilate the small sect. Henceforth the Gospel was to spread over the Western world like a prairie fire. The Palestinian confinement had burst wide open so that the formerly Jewish context of New Testament Christianity had become an imperial context. How different from the early expectation the fulfillment turned out to be! And so, we feel prompted to exclaim with the Psalmist:

Thou art the God that doest wonders. . . .

And yet, withal, the great Doer of the unexpected stands also revealed as showing forth an infinite steadiness of purpose, doing for man what man could never do for himself. As we behold over the ages the fulfillment of that Purpose, we realize that it amounts to nothing short of the salvation of the world. What the divine action discloses is an unswerving will to the good of all. Seen in this light, the whole Bible bears testimony to God's plan for restoring an originally good creation gone bad. Hence the relentless Prologue of Gen. 6:5, "The Lord saw that the wickedness of man was great in the earth, and that every imagination of the thoughts of his heart was only evil continually." Henceforth the divine judgment falls upon mortal man. Yet as the rainbow follows upon the deluge, it soon becomes clear that God's judgment is for the sake of renewal. The Gospel actually begins with Noah. The very postulation of Noah provides the clue to the "scandal of particularity," however unexpected this "scandal" may previously have appeared. The subsequent call of Abraham bears the same testimony. Truly a divine Purpose is at work in history. This is why the biblical notion of time is that of meaningful duration. The extension of the Exodus imagery to the New Testament provides a striking illustration of this. It is significant that Luke should have used the image as he reported Jesus' allusion to his "departure" to be accomplished in Jerusalem (Luke 9:31); that Paul should have carried the same interpretation when he spoke of Christ our passover in I Cor. 5:7, and further likened Christian baptism to the crossing of the Red Sea in I Cor. 10:2.

This would seem to be the pertinent place to insist that the prophetic perspective arises from a biblical interpretation of history grounded in the steadiness of God's Purpose. What is implied in the prophetic outlook is a growing awareness that events are moving in such ways as to bring about the realization of God's intended goal. Episodes are not just accidents, but happenings mediating God's will for men, and accordingly calling forth a human response amounting to righteousness. The prophetic insight leads to the conclusion that the God who thus stands at the roaring loom of history is the One who speaks, and it is done. Hence the

prophetic interpretation of history also implies a prophetic interpretation of the universe. The great prophet of the Exile, for example, reaches a climax in the exaltation of the glory and power
of the living God of Israel (Isa. 52:7–12). And the crude account
of the making of a clay model of man in the second chapter of
Genesis yields priority to the majestic opening chapter as we now
have it: "In the beginning God created the heaven and the earth.
. . ." This prophetic view further disposes of the polytheistic
Babylonian versions, for the heathen gods are ridiculed as no gods.
There is a truly biblical defiance in Isa. 41:22–24, and a terrible
finality in the conclusion, "Behold, ye are of nothing, and your
work of nought: an abomination is he that chooseth you." A new
climax is reached with the highly sarcastic evocation of a man who
fashions wood into an idolatrous representation of divinity, then
makes with the waste parts a fire to cook his meal.

Because of its steadiness, God's Purpose will never be thwarted
by human folly. Should only a handful of alerted men and women
heed the divine Imperative, the power of these few to influence
the many will be amply demonstrated. The Bible gives the lie to
the dictum that God is always on the side of the biggest battalions.

What actually hides the divine steadiness of purpose is the fact
of an infinite variety of response on the part of God. Thus, for
instance, God's response may come under the aspect of vocation,
of election, or of mission. A Samson may be given a prodigious
strength to witness for Yahweh and his people in the midst of a
degenerate and sophisticated generation succumbing to integration
by surrender to foreign influences. Or a Samuel may be given
prominence to the point of swaying the future of Israel. Again
God may be satisfied to appeal to the conscience of a people still
aware of the implications of its Covenant with him. In a more
severe vein he may prophetically convey his judgment by allowing
forebodings of trial and suffering to revive too weakened a con-

sciousness of man's obligations. Thus Isaiah's profound sense of holiness allowed him to apprehend and disclose in God's name the approaching plight of Jerusalem. Still another important form of divine response is detected in a reawakening of Israel's sense of having been marked off from a surrounding culture, as was the case when Ezekiel nurtured Hebrew ways among the Jews during their Babylonian captivity. This type of response became still more marked when the Essenes sought refuge from emperor worship in the seclusion of their communities.

The infinite variety of divine response comes within full view in the man Christ Jesus. For surely his richly shaded reactions cannot be defined by being put in the one class of "sweet reasonableness" dear to Matthew Arnold. Jesus easily disposes of the dialectical trickery of the Pharisees, and this again in a great number of ways. Now a question put to him is returned with a sharper edge. Again too Pharisaic a correctness of law or of ceremony calls forth his violent denunciation. He weeps over Jerusalem. He just looks at the backsliding Peter. He counters Pilate's sophistry with dead silence. A word or mere touch on his part mediates the unexpected ways of God's deliverance.

As Christianity begins to spread beyond the confines of the Holy Land, the infinite variety of divine response becomes more evident still. The Christ is no longer limited as he was in the days of his flesh. So also the overseas Jews are free from the narrow exclusiveness of their Jerusalem brethren. As for the Gentiles, they know of no such restrictive influences. The Gospel itself has been released from binding Hebrew connotations. It is as if God's imperatives, or at least his earnest entreaties, had become transfigured into supremely responsive ways of persuasion. Only a reverent survey of the development of hymnology and devotional classics, better still of the biographies of saintly, committed lives throughout the Christian Era, could begin to do justice to the fullness of divine response.

The unexpected character of the biblical record comes to light again and again in and through the lives of those who are committed to the Word of God, even as they express dismay or even disappointment at the ways of the great Doer of the unexpected. Yet should any man keep on contesting these ways in the face of the steadiness of a Purpose disclosed over thousands of years? Or is it not simply that the very infinity of divine forms of response exposes our human infirmity? What actually causes consternation among believers is the well-assured fact that they never can secure from God through prayer and entreaty the long-range assignment they so sorely crave. What they actually want is a blueprint for their lives, one that they can slip into their pocket and walk away with on their own.

Should this ever be the case, should this baleful privilege be granted to them, then the whole record of God's dealings with his people throughout the ages would indeed be given the lie. For if there is even one single truth this record conveys, this truth is that God never gives a blueprint to anyone. The reason for this should by now be clear to the unprejudiced reader of the Bible: the heavenly Father acts as if he did not want his own to part ways with him, to become engrossed in the glory of their own self-sufficiency until they finally end in the dejection of the far country. Quite otherwise. He wants them to grow into a loving dependence upon him, to foster in their whole being an utter trust in his infinite Providence.

A gentle lady who excelled in the conduct of spiritual retreats, the late Evelyn Underhill, once read a profound analogy in the way sheep dogs have learned to live with the shepherd in such perfect service:

They were helping the shepherd to deal with a lot of very active sheep and lambs, to persuade them into the right pastures, to keep them from rushing down the wrong paths. And how did the successful dog do it? Not by barking, fuss, ostentatious authority, any kind of busy behavior. The best dog I saw never barked once; and he spent an astonishing amount of his time sitting perfectly still, looking at the shepherd. The communion of spirit between them was perfect. They worked as a unit. Neither of them seemed anxious or in a hurry. Neither was committed to a rigid plan; they were always content to wait. That dog was the docile and faithful agent of another mind. He used his whole intelligence and initiative, but always in obedience to his master's directive will; and was ever prompt at self-effacement. The little mountain sheep he had to deal with were amazingly tiresome, as expert in doubling and twisting and going the wrong way as any naughty little boy. The dog went steadily on with it; and his tail never ceased to wag.

What did that mean? It meant that his relation to the shepherd was the centre of his life; and because of that, he enjoyed doing his job with the sheep, he did not bother about the trouble, nor get discouraged with the apparent results. The dog had transcended mere dogginess. His actions were dictated by something right beyond himself. He was the agent of the shepherd, working for a scheme which was just that which was the source of the delightedness, the eagerness, and also the discipline with which he worked. But he would not have kept that peculiar and intimate relation unless he had sat down and looked at the shepherd a good deal.[1]

That dog had adequately come to terms with the life of faith in the setting of experience and, needless to say, quite apart from any kind of theological understanding.

8

A Misplaced Rationalism Exposed

As we proceed from biblical experience to theological under-standing, a misplaced rationalism becomes our danger, a danger the Reformers early came to realize. In their apprehension of biblical realities they emulated the spirit of a modern science wary of the inflexible rationality of Aristotelian logic. Viewed in this light, both the Reformation and the new science prove to have been aspects of the same revolt. As Whitehead sees it, this revolt was essentially "an anti-intellectualist movement."[1] What stands exposed here with reference to early forms of Christian thought is a double-mindedness bent upon bridging the gap between "faith" and "reason." As Christianity had become integrated into Hellen-istic ways of thinking, the most direct, the most baleful outcome of the process had been that resulting views of God and of things Christian were bound to appear sooner or later as end products of human reasoning.

Far back in the sixth century B.C., Xenophanes of Colophon, incidentally emulating in this the Hebrew prophets, already had exposed the anthropomorphism so obviously at work in the rise of religious views as exemplified in the polytheism of Homer and Hesiod. It is so natural to mortals, he ironically satirized, to think of the gods as born the way we are and having feeling, voice, and body as we ourselves. Supposing oxen or lions could paint, they would in all probability represent their gods in the form of oxen or lions. So would Ethiopians postulate a dark-skinned type of divinity.

Yet Xenophanes did not stop at this point. Unconsciously disregarding his own warning, he proceeded to devise a divinity of his own. This divinity was indeed superior to the imaginings of the poets of ancient Greece, for it implied monotheism. His divinity was nevertheless a postulation of his own, that of one infinite being, absolute and unchangeable. His disciple Parmenides further developed and clarified the concept which Plato was to inherit. True to form, moreover, Plato early in the *Republic* took to task Homer and "the good old Hesiod" for having ascribed to the gods the most shocking and unbecoming features.[2] Plato, however, was restrained at this point by the consideration that popular religion remained the best way of keeping the rank and file under control. Accordingly his contention was that since stories about the gods must continue to be told at this "kindergarten" level, these same stories should at least be decent stories. And so it may be said that he invented theology as a protest against popular religion. By the same token he originated the concept of orthodoxy. Such an ancestry should put the zealous on their guard.

More striking still is the fact that as we come to the central books of the *Republic*,[3] the earlier "kindergarten" stage of religion has dropped out of sight. Like his masters Xenophanes and Parmenides, Plato now advocates a high religion, a religion for the elite, for what we nowadays call the intelligentsia. Through the realm of the Ideas, this high religion points to the One which puts in a late appearance in the *Parmenides,* and is henceforth well on its way to becoming Aristotle's divine self-thinking Thought, and further on Plotinus' first principle—an "it," mind you, and not a "he"—the ineffable One soon to be gratuitously identified by young Augustine as God the Father. And so it turns out that the process originated by Xenophanes, far from having "demythologized" religion, ultimately substantiated an anthropological approach to divinity at a higher level. No wonder modernity would expose again and again as mere end products of our human nature, concepts of God more or less directly derived from such anthropomorphism.

But so would far-seeing theologians, and this is the point I am anxious to make. The much maligned and greatly misunderstood Anselm of Canterbury, that truly great eleventh-century philosopher and theologian, was the first to apprehend clearly the fallacy involved in the current anthropomorphic approach. His eternal merit is to have seen that the moment a man looks upon God as a concept appearing at the far end of processes of reasoning, that is, as an end product of them, his reference is to an "it," not to him who is the Father of our Lord Jesus Christ. In other words, this kind of philosophical and religious speculation is out of touch with the living God. It misses the mark. And since the connotation of missing the mark with regard to God is that of sin, it should be conceded that the ascription of "sinner" applies to the proponents of this kind of speculation. Conversely, the theologian who has been awakened by Anselm may find himself in agreement with a well-informed modernity, for the verdict reached by both is basically the same. It amounts to saying to those who hold anthropomorphic conceptions of divinity: "Your religion is the shadow of a man unable to jump out of his own shadow. Your god is not God."

Anselm's natural bent was to allow his intellectual pilgrimage to be his prayer, and his prayer his intellectual pilgrimage. The whole first chapter of his *Proslogion* is an intensive prayer. Throughout the whole treatise, even in the midst of argument, he never departs from this attitude of worship. He sustains it to such

A MISPLACED RATIONALISM EXPOSED

a degree in fact, that he calls to mind Buber's profound dictum that "God is not to be expressed but addressed."

In this prayerful mood, then, Anselm comes to the realization that far from appearing as an end product of human thinking, God in his reality originates and conditions at every step a human thinking utterly surrendered to him. Thus Anselm opens the second chapter of the *Proslogion* ("That God truly exists") with the words: "Therefore do Thou, oh Lord, Who givest understanding of faith, grant me that . . . I may understand that Thou art as we believe [Thee to be], and Thou art that which we believe."

Here is a clear case of faith seeking understanding—an understanding of which faith is the constant and *given* presupposition. He goes on to say: "And certainly we believe that Thou art that than which no greater can be thought." Even the fool who *says* in his heart, "There is no God" (not the fool who *thinks* in his heart, "There is no God," as Bacon has pointed out in his essay "On Atheism"), even this fool understands what he hears when the preceding statement is made.[4] Thus far it may be correctly asserted that both the believer and the unbeliever share this hearing and this knowing, with the twofold result that not only is the faithful one gaining access to a fuller, more adequate faith, but the unbeliever conversely may find his foolishness fading away. Previously the unbeliever had mere head understanding of what he heard. Henceforth his whole being has been apprehended by the Reality conveyed in what he heard.

And now for an objection which well may have taken shape in the mind of some readers. "Granting all this," a man may say, "what if my faith is at so low a level that no Reality seems to be conveyed to me in what I hear?" And further, "How can I be sure that all that I am told about Reality is not to be ascribed to my own subjectivity, that is, to my wishful thinking?" The relevance of this objection was so obvious to Anselm that his whole treatise may be interpreted as a tentative answer to it. I say "tentative," not "final," because the Reality under consideration can never be an object of formal demonstration. Should it be made to appear in this light, we would *ipso facto* revert to the very illusion Anselm started out to expose in the first place. And the way he went about doing this, his *Proslogion,* was by asking how human thought can ever grasp a Reality admittedly beyond human reach. The opening pages of his *Epistola de Incarnatione Verbi* further point to an Anselm increasingly aware that it is preposterous to aim at ascending by reason alone to the position held by faith. Clearly, an understanding without faith cannot achieve this.

Withal, the Anselm of *Proslogion* knows to what extent even a believer of infinite goodwill may yet feel remote from the living God. There is an aching note of pathos in his outcry, "If Thou art everywhere, why do I not see Thee present? . . . I strove toward God, and I stumbled but on myself." A reader familiar with this paradox in the life of faith may well ask, Could it be that God who so readily helps steady our first steps, later allows us to falter on our own so as to instill in us a still greater dependence on him? So it would seem. Anselm himself envisages again and again the vicissitudes of a pilgrimage under low ceiling. Yet the point is that he remains aware of them always in the context of faith. In him the feeling of an absence never amounts to an absence of feeling. And lo and behold, as we reach chapter 26 in the *Proslogion,* the mood of quiet desperation is transfigured into one of heavenly joy—"an abundance, yes! and a superabundance."

So it appears that the appeal to God which mounts up from the second to the twenty-fifth chapters like a crescendo of Handel, or perhaps still more like the great waters of one of Bach's preludes, has actually involved a growing divine disclosure climaxing in the Self-giving of the Presence. Whoever will heed this category of Presence in Scripture—if I may use this terribly inadequate word "category" to suggest the Reality I have in mind—is faced by one of the most fascinating studies a plain man could ever undertake. For this is the way to read the great pages of the Bible, as they bring God closer to one.

It is noteworthy that Anselm wrote the *Monologion* unwillingly. In its Prologue he is at pains to explain that those who constrained him to undertake this work laid upon him the condition that he should not take argument from the authority of Scripture, but proceed in all simplicity according to well-established methods of reasoning to the point where his case should become incontrovertible. This unwholesome prescription he fulfilled to the letter, and it is this docility and goodwill on his part which has lent motive to shortsighted criticism.

Let us take a still closer look. Indeed through seventy-nine chapters Anselm draws upon neither Scripture nor Christian doctrine. It is only when we come to the eightieth chapter that we are made to realize that even the most helpful rational argument cannot provide the adequate ground upon which the true God can be conclusively identified. The issue henceforth comes to a head in the question, How did he achieve this? And the obvious answer is, by means of a dialectical method now found to have been at work throughout the incriminated treatise. And this method is grounded in the *Proslogion*. It is the method of faith seeking understanding. We are consequently forced to the conclusion that a work undertaken by him against his own inclination has, from beginning to end, afforded the good and faithful servant with one more opportunity to vindicate the Christian faith in the face of unbelief. A previous feeling of regret on our part may well turn to one of gratitude toward those who thought evil against Anselm, for by their attempt we are able to ascertain Anselm's real significance.

Let us insist that Anselm aimed essentially at showing that any concept of God which appears at the terminal of a process of reasoning is not necessarily God, but may be rightly considered as a mere product of our human nature. It is a fact that in the measure to which the Anselmian case against the anthropological approach has been lost sight of, the detractors of Christianity have held the field, with a further resulting loss on their part of a sense of ultimate purpose.

This situation has come to a climax in our time, and only a recovery of the Anselmian insight has allowed theology to meet it. It will readily appear that the best vantage point for a pertinent evaluation of the issue at hand is the position taken by Karl Barth in his critique of Schleiermacher.

9

The Barthian Critique of Schleiermacher

My intention is not to write under this title a dissertation on the theology of Karl Barth as contrasted with that of Schleiermacher in order to ascertain the respective merit of each. This task may be left safely in the hands of Paul Tillich, who has good reasons to be interested in it. Better still, this larger, exhaustive treatment may be entrusted to Karl Barth himself if we are to judge by his masterly and profoundly honest treatment of Schleiermacher in *Die Protestantische Theologie im Neunzehnten Jahrhundert*, truly the work of a Christian gentleman.[1]

The Barthian critique of Schleiermacher[2] is of interest to us at this point only insofar as it sheds light on the subject at hand. For this same reason we see no necessity for recounting the spiritual and intellectual pilgrimage of Barth from nineteenth-century liberalism to the radically Christocentric views now unfolding in his *Die Kirchliche Dogmatik*. This, incidentally, has been done over and over again. It may be taken for granted, therefore, that this aspect of the subject is familiar to the reader.

The main point at issue is that Karl Barth increasingly has been led to detect in Schleiermacher's views, the modern archetype of the anthropological approach to theology—an approach, that is, whereby the pious self-consciousness of the religious man has usurped the place which rightly belongs to the sovereign and unconditionally prior Word of God. Implied in Schleiermacher's anthropological method, as Barth sees it, is the presupposition that man may derive a valid knowledge of God from his own concepts, ultimately from his own certainty. In Schleiermacher Barth identifies a spiritual descendant of Descartes. With unswerving logic he exposes in the latter's *cogito ergo sum* (I think, therefore I am) the perennial principle according to which the theology of the Word of God reasserted by the Protestant Reformation has been reduced to anthropology.[3] According to Barth, however, there is no way from anthropology to Christology. There is only a way from Christology to anthropology. God is known only through God. This authentic knowledge can only be the knowledge of faith, a knowledge energized and conditioned at every step by a sovereign and utterly prior Word.

The theme already has become so familiar to the reader that there is no need to labor its connotations. Yet this same familiarity invites further inquiry. How did Karl Barth come to the conviction that the standpoint of Schleiermacher summed up the position he, Karl Barth, must oppose? In his anxiety to reassert the priority of the Word of God over against the word of man, Barth had been led in earlier days to expose the deceptive character of the solipsism inherent in all forms of idealism. With this in mind, he had most naturally turned to Kierkegaard as to the great challenger of Hegel. Yet in the long run he could not fail to realize that Kierkegaard's existentialism, in spite of its high dialectical quality, still implied in more than one way an experiential method taking man as a starting point.

The crux of the difficulty then was the experiential method *per se,* and Barth realized it early in his new career. Yet it was only after he had come to find Schleiermacher the incarnation of all that the experiential method stood for, that he was enabled to define his own Christology in its fullness. Once more in his case, contradiction at a specific point proves to have forced theological clarification. To be sure, Barth had good reasons to be familiar with the lifework of Schleiermacher. Yet it was not until Emil Brunner sharpened his own case against Schleiermacher that Barth was made aware of the possibilities of this kind of theology in reverse. Henceforth necessity was laid upon him to set himself against the stream of two hundred years of Protestant theology. This is more easily said than done. How would Barth set about it? The answer was provided thanks to an amazing insight into the true perspective of theological thought throughout the ages.

One of the many merits—I should probably say, blessings—of Karl Barth is his rediscovery of Anselm. This rediscovery came to light with the publication in Munich, 1931, of *Fides Quaerens Intellectum, Anselm's Beweis der Existenz Gottes* (Faith seeking understanding, Anselm's proof of the existence of God). A common friend who used to take long walks with Barth during those Munich days has given me a vivid impression of the atmosphere of near romance that pervaded this rediscovery of Anselm. There was in it the profound joy of the Pilgrim who at long last had reached the Interpreter's house, sure to find there the answers relating to the way he must go. It should be noted at this point that the following year (1932) Barth felt constrained to break with existentialism.[4]

The importance of Barth's rediscovery of Anselm can hardly be exaggerated. The Swiss theologian looms over the intervening ages as the true heir to the medieval master. Yet it remains for Anselm to take the measure of Barth, whose dogmatic interpretation of the *credo ut intelligam* (I believe so that I may understand) fails at times to heed the creative flexibility of Anselm, especially with regard to the influence that the intellection of faith exerts upon faith itself. In his anxiety to show that Anselm is not a "natural theologian," Barth is carried to extremes of self-contradiction. He forgets, for instance, that he himself has emphasized the fact that Anselm does not argue from the authoritative "givenness" of Scripture or creed, to dogmatic conclusions.

The reason for these extremes seems twofold, as I see it: Barth has an ax to grind, and he proceeds mostly in his individual solitude. As John Henry Newman has pointed out, solitary individuals may contribute to the advance of knowledge, but it is better for the cause of knowledge that they should not be solitary, since truth is wrought out by many minds freely working together. It is noteworthy that when Newman expressed these views as points of contrast between the Church of his day and the primitive Church, he could do so only because he was fresh from the study of the Fathers. His remark may well be an incentive for Christians to do likewise.

Just as it remains for Anselm to take the measure of Barth, it would seem to have remained for Barth to take the measure of "modernism." This he has done in recent years by devising an Anselmian type of approach to the subject. Anselmian insights have become clues to the evaluation of a Schleiermacher acknowledged as the great modern formulator of anthropocentric theology and in this capacity the founder not of a school but of an age, as Barth frankly admits.

The standpoint of Schleiermacher leads him to emphasize a divine immanence stirring up within man a pious (*fromm*) feeling of absolute dependence upon the Infinite. Hence the mystical experience of apprehending delicate vibrations (*Gemüt*) which harmonized in his case with the inwardness of the Moravians.[5] So did it, incidentally, with a prevalent mood of romanticism. Soon Tieck and Novalis would suggest the same experience in terms of an inner music. In the same vein William James would suggest an intimate sense of "companionship" with the invisible through

[88]

the analogy of a quiet music playing in the back of his mind. A Mendelssohn might well characterize that music as being "without words."

This would be just as well for Schleiermacher and his followers since an emphasis on religious experience together with its projections in symbol and myth, implies a corresponding minimization of dogma, or at least an admission of the relativity of dogma. For in the new context dogma is merely the language spoken by faith, a language conditioned by an ever-changing social and cultural determinism. As a result the place previously occupied by dogma is taken by a critical history of dogma, and at this point conflicts between science and theology lose their sting. Another corollary of the anthropocentric approach is an emphasis on God as Spirit, the stirrings of the Holy Spirit being commensurate with the potentialities of the human subject. "God-certainty" becomes the illusory "self-certainty" of a subject henceforth prisoner of his own subjectivity.

In setting himself up against the stream, Barth constantly labors against the temptation of establishing the unconditional priority of a sovereign God by asserting the nothingness of man without God. In spite of all that has been held against Barth on this count, intellectual honesty compels one to admit that our theologian remains constantly aware of the existence and dignity of man, and this in two ways at least. He knows in the first place that man has the alternative of resisting the grace of God, together with the power to do so. In withstanding he stands, and this undeniable fact establishes that of his existence. As for man's dignity, it is involved in this very faculty to rebel. It is the dignity of a sinner henceforth led astray to the point of becoming a traitor to himself. This is admittedly a questionable kind of dignity, but it remains a dignity nevertheless because its ultimate reference is to

God. It is in the last analysis, then, the dignity of a creature aware of its creatureliness.[6]

The mastery of Barth, coming as it does to full expression in his monumental *Die Kirchliche Dogmatik*, is that of a great musical composer who practices to perfection the art of working into a leading theme, parts which harmonize with it and are at the same time intrinsically melodious. Neither is he satisfied with single counterpoint. Again and again he freely engages in invertible counterpoint. In the instance now under consideration, we may follow the details of the theological development in terms of double counterpoint. In so doing we may realize the meticulous care with which Barth has worked out a well-nigh perfect parallelism between the two lines of consideration just emphasized with reference to the existence and dignity of man.

According to Barth man has been made aware of his existence, that is, of his faculty to stand in revolt, in the measure to which he has been enabled to probe his real nature with reference to that of the perfectly obedient Christ. It is in the Savior that a man may discern the perfect expression of God's grace, and by the same token begin to take the measure of his own sin as a counterpart of God's grace. In the same breath, as it were, this man's understanding of himself ceases to be anthropocentric, becoming instead theocentric as his call and election in Jesus Christ take on reality. And it is all the work of God through the Holy Spirit now an "it" no longer, but *He,* the prior, sovereign God.

In the theological consideration of an anthropology derived from Christology, and as such proceeding in the light and energizing power of faith in the Covenanter God, the circle of mere human self-understanding has been broken.[7] Man, the truth of man, has been once for all determined by God in Christ. This is the reason Barth asserts that while there is no way from anthropology to a genuine theology of the Word, there *is* a way from this theology to anthropology. We may characterize it as the way of the Theological Man.

And so the crucial weakness detected by Barth in the anthropology of Schleiermacher is that it concerns only the Phenomenal Man, not the real man. The same critique extends *a fortiori* to all scientific and secular disciplines, insofar as they concern themselves with phenomena as viewed by Everyman. Admittedly, the work they do is useful because it implies seeing, foreseeing, and providing for existence at the human level of existence. This is especially the case for scientific anthropology. It gathers together and organizes an amazing mass of data with a view to orienting and bettering our everyday life in the economic and social realms. There is definitely a place for cultural activities of this sort. Such activities, however, must further be characterized by a radical inability to tell the ultimate truth about the world of nature and of man.[8] Indeed they actually hide God and the things which are God's, that is, everything that truly matters. Apart from the life of faith, man sees nothing aright.

With reference to the loss by modern man of a sense of cosmic purpose, it is not difficult to see what Barth would be likely to answer to a man like Professor W. T. Stace of Princeton, and especially to his *Atlantic Monthly* article, "Man Against Darkness," quoted in our first chapter. If I may be bold enough to put words under the pen of Karl Barth, they would declare in substance: "What you say is perfectly true, Professor. Modern man has lost a sense of cosmic purpose, has lost view of his only and true purpose which is literally God in Christ, God the Word. And you are right again in saying that this happened, at least as seen from the surface at our secular level, through the agency of science. The reason for this is that restricting itself to the outlook of the natural man, however perfected the methods, science has *ipso facto* drawn above and around modern man, and more especially within him, the thickest Iron Curtain that ever was under God's high heaven. Hence ultimately, the sort of thing referred to, and rightly so, as the nonreferential character of uninterpreted formalisms." Whereupon the Swiss theologian, who is at heart an evangelist, might press God's case and add in the next breath, "Let faith therefore open your eyes that you may be granted the freedom to see and understand aright. Heed the Gospel!"

As I was giving free play to my thoughts, I fancied I saw Bertrand Russell in some kind of Mephistophelic garb peeping in from behind the scene; then as he turned aside I overheard his remark, "And so I do not see anything aright? Or do I?"

Whether or not imagination in this case proved once more to have been a "queen of lies and error" is not for me to say. Of this I am sure, however: the question at hand is not only pertinent, but it is the most pressing question of which one can think at this point.

PART III

Points of Contact
Between Modern Science and Theology

10

A Common Indictment
of Anthropomorphism

THE mental picture of Karl Barth's Phenomenal Man does not suggest the man "of flesh and bones" dear to Miguel de Unamuno, any more than that of the Economic Man postulated a century ago, or of the Primitive Man constructed by our professional anthropologists. And yet these constructs have proved fruitful of further findings. Again, in a different line of consideration, the scientist who does his best to dodge the deceptions of the human recording set by substituting mechanical and other corrective devices for the classical stargazer, merely aims at improving the observation and interpretation of data. The same criterion applies to the use of a symbolic logic meant to do away with a personal equation likely to deflect trends of thought proceeding along empirical lines of approach.

In all such cases, although to a much lesser degree, what Barth characterizes as the Phenomenal Man is actually taken to task. The point I am anxious to make, however, is that an enlightened modernity has already gone a long way in exposing this Phenomenal Man and his anthropomorphic ways. The advances of contemporary theology merely amount to catching up with modernity, though for infinitely better reasons. For surely anthropomorphism does far more mischief in theology than in the other sciences. Thus it appears that both an enlightened modernity and an enlightened Christianity are steering their respective courses in the same direction.

This unexpected aspect of the situation has not as yet received the attention it would seem to deserve, mostly on account of deep-seated prejudices. As a result the pot has been calling the kettle black. The time has come to bring to a head some of our previous conclusions, and allow them to shed more light on the issue as exemplified at the close of the preceding chapter in an innocent witticism on Bertrand Russell. We shall do so by considering the true impact of the Anselm-inspired approach of Barth on the one hand, and on the other a modern approach increasingly wary of the empirical, anthropomorphic data of the consciousness.

According to Barth, the Phenomenal Man is not the true man. There is a radical irrelevancy in his methods. They cannot lead him to a true knowledge of God. Hence the ever-recurring theme: There is no way from anthropology to the theology of the Word of God. The amazing thing about all anthropocentric approaches to God is that they hide a multiplicity of fallacies. In the first place, their ultimate reference is not to God, but to a man-made concept of God. They prove particularly deceptive when they proceed under the cover of orthodoxy to propound a literalism bordering on idolatry, if not on absurdity. The words said to have been conveyed in terms of verbal inspiration, all of them, actually need to be tested in their differentiation from the Word of God, Jesus Christ, as well as in their possible relationship to him. Similarly, so-called fundamental doctrines are inconclusive, in fact without foundation apart from those independent, primary insights directly mediated in any act of God together with the standards for judging them. Acts of God happen along an ever-moving biblical line, as a trail suggestive of God's time is blazed from one hallowed spot to the other. By virtue of their divine origin, however, these acts of God do not essentially belong in any psychological or objectively historical (*historisch*) setting. For these reasons they may indeed have to be characterized and interpreted in unusual ways. Should we then try to make them more accessible by means of reinterpretation, allegory, metaphor, symbol, type, or figure, the outcome would merely be doctrines of man's own making, and ultimately anthropomorphic world views.

Condemned by the same token is the liberal approach to "religion" through psychology and history, as both these scientific disciplines proceed upon the immediate data of consciousness of the Phenomenal Man. According to Barth, these data cannot become a source of the knowledge of God because it is God who defines man, and not the other way around. To define any object is to put it in a class, while God is One by himself. Therefore, all attempts to reverse the God-given process of adequate knowledge merely emphasize the alienation of a creature in contradiction. Strictly speaking, the truth of God in Christ is both nonpsychological and nonhistorical. What has misled the Phenomenal Man to think otherwise is that the events characterized as acts of God are ultimately recorded in human nature within the roaring loom of history. This, however, cannot be construed as implying that either human nature or a historical sequence can become approaches to God. Indeed the contrary is true. It is God who takes the measure of both, without being ultimately conditioned by them. Let us frankly admit, therefore, that historical criticism as we know it becomes irrelevant to the degree to which it mostly concerns itself with the facts that can be empirically ascertained. Hence a new approach must be devised to the experiential (*geschichtlich*) data pertaining to evangelical history, as contrasted to objectively historical (*historisch*) data. That Barth is keenly aware of this need becomes ever more apparent as *Die Kirchliche Dogmatik* unfolds.

It now appears that current psychological and historical categories cannot convey the true nature and implications of events originating in the free and sovereign grace of God. The fact that these events are ultimately recorded in human nature within the canvas of history does not make them psychological or historical in the sense currently ascribed to these words. All that may fairly be stated is that they are events pertaining to the innermost life of the Israel of God, of the Body of Christ. Provided no connotation of "progressive revelation" be read into this interpretation, it may further be said that throughout the ages the People of God have thought aloud the acts of God after him. It is in this context that Barth writes theology in terms of the affirmations of the Church, in terms of *Church* dogmatics.

What then is the pristine "given" upon which this reconceived theology originally proceeds? Or, to put the question in another way, How can the theologian do without the usual categories of psychology and history? Barth's over-all answer is that the theologian will find the pristine "given" hidden away behind, and conversely mediated through, the history of the Covenant relationship between God and man. And further, that the touchstone of a biblical truth grounded in the reliability of God is the Word of God himself, Jesus Christ. This answer admittedly raises an awe-inspiring question: How is the theologian to know and interpret Jesus Christ, if not through a critical assessment using the methods of psychology and of history? Let it be realized that asking the question in these terms amounts to reverting to the age-old anthropocentric illusion exposed through the preceding pages.

The main point to keep in mind is that the possibility of any solution lies in the freedom and sovereignty of God's grace and initiative, in this case in the fact of his condescending abasement.

In Jesus Christ, God enters our world by assuming a form known to man, that of a servant. In this manner he encounters man where man is in such a way that man may understand him. And it is only in and through this event we call incarnation that the truth about man is known in judgment and renewal. Henceforth a man may become through God's free and sovereign grace an adopted son remade in the image of the eternal Son. And so the Word of God has ceased to be bound to any biblical literature or written confession, although the value of both is still acknowledged in terms of standard and guidance. There and then the Scripture is fulfilled as true manhood stands revealed.

This is likely to become more evident still if we consider the ways in which Barth henceforth proceeds to construct his theology of the Word. Our best standpoint for such a consideration is the very center of his theology—namely, his Christology. Christology has ceased to proceed upon the "Jesus of history." As Barth sees it, the Gospels have never been meant to provide a source for knowledge about the man from Nazareth. No wonder, therefore, that so much skepticism is possible with regard to the kind of human personality Jesus actually was, to the point that any interest in the question may be excluded. Barth is not likely to be upset by the negative assertions of such Form critics as Professor R. H. Lightfoot. I refer to the widely quoted statement with which the latter concluded his Bampton Lectures, *History and Interpretation in the Gospels:* "For all the inestimable value of the Gospels, they yield us little more than a whisper of his voice: we trace in them but the outskirts of his ways."[1] Barth goes even further than this. As Kierkegaard has taught him to see it, should a professional historian gain access to the human career of Jesus, the result would prove most disappointing to him, for he would be confronted only by a divine incognito, a veiling of God.[2] Even for those who met Jesus in the days of his flesh, he did not become a revelation. It is only in his office as Revealer and Reconciler, as God in a human mode of existence, that he meets man in judgment and renewal. In other words he is not of God as creatures are of God. Otherwise his office would be an event within this created, fallen order—a vain event. All in all, Jesus has no real human existence apart from his office, and his existence is given with this office.[3]

Let me make it clear that in the present chapter thus far I have not attempted to judge the views of Karl Barth. I have merely tried to bring out, with reference to the most influential theologian of our time, the basic implication of the present-day reorientation of theology—namely, an increasing awareness of the misleading character of anthropocentric, empirical views proceeding upon the data of human consciousness.

The insight on which theology is beginning to proceed in all earnestness has long become commonplace in modernity. To it modern science in particular may be said to owe most of its originality and fruitfulness, as entire sections of the present work have already pointed out. This is to say that modernity would have no difficulty in admitting with Karl Barth that anthropocentric views proceeding from mere experience and intruding into a man's reasoning are likely to lead to illusory knowledge. Nor would it hesitate to grant that only as man-made notions are brought under control can the mind profitably proceed toward the reality impinging on it.

Had this situation been better appraised, a great deal of vain as well as unchristian denunciation and name-calling might have been avoided. So also fruitful exchange of views between Christianity and modernity might have taken place among men of goodwill. With reference to the question asked for the sake of argument at the end of our previous chapter, it should be granted that a Bertrand Russell apprehends aright an impressive area of knowledge.

There is deep meaning in Emil Brunner's seemingly trivial remark that it would be meaningless to speak of Christian mathematics. His reference is to the disturbance likely to be brought about by sin in rational knowledge. He sees it at its maximum in the human and theological sciences which bring the scholar closer to that center of existence where knowledge concerns questions of values such as our conceptions of freedom, of the good community, and ultimately of man's relations to God. The farther away the matter under consideration lies from this center, the less the disturbance due to sin. The minimum is registered in the exact sciences and ultimately reaches the zero point in the sphere of the formal.[4]

Insofar, therefore, as a Bertrand Russell busies himself with forms of symbolic logic wherein logic and extremely abstract forms of mathematics are fused into one single, formal, nonreferential discipline bereft of any empirical content, his activity is fully valid. It is indeed as perfectly regulated and potentially useful as can be. It evades the disturbance ascribable to sin as surely as the laws of field physics become invariant with respect to the Lorentz transformation, or as there exists an ideal C. S. (co-ordinate system) from which the laws of mechanics are universally valid. This state of things applies to all uninterpreted formalisms. Karl Barth himself should concede this much as he increasingly assumes responsibility for the cultural situation of our time.

But to admit this much does not imply that the certification of the human mind stops right there at the frontiers of the strictly formal. Even as we proceed toward that center of existence where man's relation to God becomes more marked, a certain degree of generalized certification remains possible. This is true in the case of such disciplines as chemistry and even biology. It becomes less so in such human sciences as the psychological and the historical. It would seem, therefore, that the neutral ground of knowledge where believers and nonbelievers can meet tends to shrink to an ever-narrower ledge as the disturbance ascribable to sin is more keenly felt.

By the same token the misleading character of anthropomorphic views and methods is bound to become more manifest as the inquiry penetrates the realm of the human and theological sciences. And yet this happens to be the very realm where the mischief has been less noted thus far. Here also the mathematical and natural sciences have shown the way. Early in their development they have realized the extent to which a gratuitous finalism has interfered again and again with a painstaking induction.

In his philosophical tale, *Candide,* Voltaire has freely caricatured the optimism of those who argue, for example, that human beings have been provided with noses because spectacles had to be worn by so many people. It is further a fact that one of his contemporaries seriously maintained that melons show divisions because they are meant to be shared in a family circle. By reading back into phenomena their own notion of purpose, however childish or rudimentary, well-meaning people have undeniably interfered with an earnest scientific quest. As a result science has turned against this kind of projection.

At a more advanced stage, scholars have realized that the scale of observation goes a long way in determining phenomena. Thus what the naked eye identifies as the nose of a statue becomes at the microscopic scale a broken yet still solid line; at the chemical scale it turns into a conglomeration of atoms; under the electron microscope it is pronounced a teeming mass of energy quanta.

What is true of the microcosm is just as true of the realm of astrophysics where the data gathered by the human eye have proved increasingly erroneous. Hence the astronomer looking through a telescope has become a legendary character. Most of the work of our gigantic telescopes is now done by photography, better still by means of motion pictures. Thus movies of the prominences of the sun are daily taken from the towers of the McMath-Hulbert Observatory at Lake Angelus, Michigan. Similarly the Harvard Observatory has been equipped with a coronograph by means of which the solar corona may be seen without waiting for a total eclipse of the sun.

Behind these and similar innovations we may detect a growing determination to eliminate the misleading human recording set. Instruments are further called upon to correct chances of error due to other causes. The Schmidt cameras, for instance, which take in large areas of the sky, have a correcting plate of thin glass placed at the front of the telescope. Last but not least, observations made in increasingly depersonalized ways are essentially meant to test mental constructions devised in terms of "useful fiction," that is, of models depersonalized to the point of competing for the title of "happy symbols." These relational structures may be said to be more about themselves than about nature proper. As the ledge of the knowable narrows down, the dead end of the nonreferential is reached.

As a result of these and similar developments and of their many ramifications, we witness on every hand a progressive elimination of the anthropocentric standpoint and line of approach. It would seem to be true, then, that in both the theological and the nontheological realms, the further from the man-made empirical data of consciousness this progressive elimination has led the inquirer, the closer and the truer the resulting approximation has proved.

The way has henceforth been opened to a more adequate understanding of human knowledge in terms of events breaking in on their own and amounting to a process of revelation.

11

The Wider Meaning of Revelation

F AR-SEEING theologians have shown us that the determination of a Christian's status under God bears profound analogy to the determination of truth in the environment of the genuine scientist.

In both cases an external reality is involved, a reality which breaks in upon a man without any manifest design on his part. In every case, moreover, the reality involved has not previously been considered, at least in terms of the features ultimately ascribed to it after it had come within view. The best one comes to know about this reality is that it was *there* in the first place, and then literally "happened" to him.

The history of the rise of man and conversely that of great inventions and discoveries is rich in illustrations of this fundamental order. Think, for example, of the birth of language, or of what James H. Breasted has called in a great title *The Dawn of Conscience;* again, of the invention of printing or the discovery of America. Call to mind the dramatic circumstances in the midst of which Archimedes gained access to the general principle of hydrostatics, or Newton to the law of gravitation. Or remember the great mathematician Henri Poincaré greeted by what he called "the mother-idea" of a mathematical solution just as he was getting into his carriage. Does not the process involved in any such happening truly amount to a *revelation,* and should we not accordingly stretch the meaning of this word to take in the new connotation? The process under consideration of course comes to a climax in the now familiar biblical notion of truth as encounter, as exemplified in Saul's confrontation by the living Christ on the road to Damascus. We already have pointed in this light to God as the great Doer of the unexpected. Clearly what comes to the awareness of the faithful with regard to the Creator also comes to the awareness of those eager minds concerned with the understanding of the works of creation, and it is one and the same process which is basically involved in these many aspects of disclosure. This world in which we live may be likened to a great signaling station. Our main task in this life is to try to make out its meaning, proceeding at all times upon what we have learned. This task and vocation implies a universal call.

I am more especially anxious to show that this notion of knowledge as happening, together with its corollaries, implies a common ground where Christianity and modernity can meet and remain on speaking terms. Because genuine knowledge involves essentially that which happens to us, it stands to reason that the Anselmian method is susceptible of generalization inasmuch as it implies a caveat against all forms of man-made knowledge, against concepts merely spun out of the human self.

To say this is to expose afresh Descartes' so-called *faux pas* which essentially implied reading Anselm out of context. For the moment Descartes attempted to infer the existence of God from the prior evidence of his own thinking in a context bereft of faith, he did the very thing Anselm had warned against. In view of this one should agree with William Temple's indictment of the new departure. The doubt Descartes indulged in while meditating in his famous "stove" was preposterous since he was as sure of the existence of the "stove" as he was of his own. Knowledge of the world around us is far more rudimentary than knowledge of self. To say the least, our knowledge of the world is not more inferential than the knowledge of our own existence. It is fair to state, then, that the author of the *Discourse on Method* found the wrong residuum. I subscribe to the contention of the late Archbishop of Canterbury—upon whom the blessing of Anselm seems to have come—that the residuum Descartes ought to have reached was the subject-object relationship. It is noteworthy that F. H. Heinemann has suggested the substitution of *Respondeo ergo sum* (I respond, therefore I am) for Descartes' *Cogito ergo sum* (I think, therefore I am). This at least would add the human faculty of reacting to events, that is, of making decisions, to that of merely thinking. We should go further yet and face up to the whole of the event, that is, to the event together with its aftermath. Thus Rosenstock-Huessy has proposed the further corrective, *Respondeo etsi mutabor* (I respond, although I shall be changed). We are dealing here with human beings, not with

> The unmotivated herd that only sleep and feed.

We have previously acknowledged the priority of a will-to-live constantly threatened one way or another. Indeed men have to fight hard to maintain themselves on the narrow ledge of existence, and if possible improve their hold upon it in terms of freedom. This implies co-operation with their fellow men. Their contention is with both the ever-recurring possibilities of nonexistence, and the temptation of adaptation through slavish surrender to their environment, physical or social. Organic solidarity is the natural solution to their plight. In a culture in normal transition, solidarity will be wrought out in actual practice before its ways are analyzed and codified. This, of course, does not mean that analysis and codification once having intervened will not help in the orientation of the process involved—namely, that of the division of social labor.

The functional development of human cultures actually proceeded in dialectical ways long before the ways of dialectics had come to any degree of expression. Contradiction acts at once as an enemy and as a friendly stimulus, whether in conversation, in everyday happenings, or in the scientific practice of statement and restatement. The reason dialectics has developed into a mental process of the first order is that contradiction is inherent in the world of nature and of man.

In its endless contention with this world, thought has emerged through an accumulation of racial memories pertaining to an infinity of happenings and to the ways in which these events have been handled. The events in turn have shaped and reshaped the human mind which had wrought out decisions in the midst of strife. It should be noted that in actual practice the word "decision" applies to positive result before it does to a fixed intention. Viewed in this way the human mind bears a witness similar to that of gills, of feet, and of prehensile toes in the story of evolution. So does a culture, as Jacob Burckhardt has shown in his insistence upon the spontaneous character of its emergence through advances of material life. A culture accordingly appears to Malinowski as an artificial secondary environment superposed on the natural. Even under this aspect, however, it constitutes a reality *sui generis* made up of a solid heritage of artifacts, technical processes, and acknowledged values, together with customs, habits, beliefs, and of course language.[1] This is why the best approach to the understanding of culture is the functional approach. Of course no materialistic connotation is implied in this last statement. What is implied is that cultural values are developed from a constant confrontation with the realities of material and social life in the context of environment.

Our next step is to realize that this is true at all levels. It is a fact, for example, that the Christian faith has been most clearly defined at the points at which "heretics" have concentrated their attacks. To be sure, values are increasingly cultivated for their own sake as well as for the sake of action. The human awareness of purpose, for instance, arises from contradiction because it cannot tolerate contradiction, and it moves from incoherence to precariousness only to find more incoherence to remove. One of the reasons for the weakness of modernity's sense of purpose today comes within view at this point—namely, that our thinking as a whole has become too formal, too artificial. Western man still finds it difficult to surrender the old illusion that "truths" are the end products of his own speculation. His mind remains that of a pseudo-maker rather than of a genuine knower. Such is the legacy of hopelessly anthropomorphic ways of reasoning, a legacy which has reappeared in a Cartesian method unable to emerge from the realm of subjectivity under the creative impact of the reality constantly impinging upon it. This anthropological solipsism comes to full expression in the Kantian "Copernican revolution" wherein the pseudo-making process already exposed blazes the trail for the Hegelian dramatization of dialectics for their own sake.

I have come to believe that the lack of realism exhibited by a great deal of the academic thinking current in our times has helped bring about a dangerous mental and spiritual vacuum. It has done so because of an inherent solipsism which has caused it to become immune to the realities which constantly impinge upon it. I further believe that the impact Marx, Engels, and their followers have made down to this day, such a propitious vacuum helping, must be ascribed to a contrasting impression of realism conveyed by the materialistic overtone of their dialectical approach. The reason there was a ring of truth in *The Communist Manifesto*[2] is that it seemed to hammer out its propositions from highly colored historical happenings; and further, that the new proclamation was made to give the lie to the Apostolic Proclamation then so weakly held that it was no longer heard. All the "prisoners of starvation" henceforth knew was that it merely meant "pie in the sky when you die."

This much is sure: such a challenge as that of Communism today cannot be met by the type of sheer counterpropaganda exemplified by "The Voice of America." Neither can we afford to ignore it by hiding our heads in the sand. We must cope with it. Once more I find myself in agreement with the late Archbishop of Canterbury. Said William Temple in his Gifford Lectures delivered in Glasgow, 1932–34, under the title *Nature, Man and God:*

> I believe that the Dialectical Materialism of Marx, Engels and Lenin has so strong an appeal to the minds of many of our contemporaries, and has so strong a foundation in contemporary experience, that only a Dialectic more comprehensive in its range of apprehension and more thorough in its appreciation of the interplay of factors in the real world, can overthrow it or seriously modify it as a guide to action.[3]

What thoughtful people want, what they need, is a sense of REALITY. To say that they are losing a sense of ultimate purpose is to imply that they have become impervious to the Word of God, just as truly as to say of sophisticated people that their having lost this or that specific sense of obligation implies that they have become impervious to the same. When Karl Barth insists that God is only known through God, he is pointing to one aspect—and by far the most important—of a universal order according to which knowledge of an object is the specific determination by that object of certain features pertaining to the existence of the knowing subject.

All genuine knowledge is revelation, a disclosure in which the object is essentially the addresser and the subject essentially the addressee. Even this tree is only known through this tree by one who is interested in trees. Only a failure to heed the wider aspect of the human situation can explain a radical unwillingness ever to look upon the scientific knowledge of nature as a mode of divine self-disclosure. In very much the same manner the impassible viewer of a painting of Van Gogh is denied the faculty of securing real insight into the personality and true genius of the artist.

In all these instances the right interpretation of the object is conditioned by the absence, or the presence, or the degree of responsiveness in the subject. A man is bound to remain impervious to the ultimate truth of Jesus Christ if he is not arrested by the active power of the living God conveyed in and through the particular events which a reverent, genuine scholarship ascertains about our Lord. Again an unbeliever may fail to identify the living God in and through the works of Creation if the energizing might of the Creator remains a dead letter to him. Indeed he may even deny any cosmic character to the universe or doubt its objective reality altogether if the world of nature does not speak to his condition, that is, if the only landscape accessible to him does not imply an objective order of reality. How may he then reverse his course and gain access to the fullness of the truth if not through a method informed from the approach Anselm so powerfully advocated?

The way to renewal will remain blocked as long as it is believed that man is endowed with a seemingly inexhaustible faculty to spin reality out of his own substance. To keep on believing this amounts to entertaining the anthropological illusion exposed by Anselm and revitalized by Descartes. Now the time has come to acknowledge that this is the very illusion which Bertrand Russell, and in his wake the representatives of symbolic logic, have themselves both surrendered and exposed in admitting to the colorless

and ultimately nonreferential character of their mental constructions. In so doing they happen to have cleared our path. And this
is why we can "do business with them," learn from them, and put
to good use what we have learned as these pages are trying to do.
As I have come to see it, this attitude on our part, together with
the policy it implies, is wiser and certainly more Christian than
avoidance and name-calling.

We are now in a better position to realize that the issue involved in wondering as to what a man can believe, or whether he
can believe at all, is not essentially one of content. Neither has it
anything to do with the converse criterion of the permissible in
terms of human experience. Quite the opposite. In all the occurrences involved, the origin of current misgivings and misunderstandings should be traced to another source—namely, to an
anthropocentric outlook bent upon producing both truth and
criterion of truth. For such an outlook not only ignores the fact
that knowledge is essentially happening in which a given reality
breaks in upon the knower, but it blocks the path to what actually
amounts to a process of revelation.

12

Revelation and Degrees of Response

THE reason man-made truth is essentially irrelevant now becomes clear to the point of triviality. Reality breaks in upon man mostly apart from any manifest design on his part. As a result he does not make the truth. He is confronted by happenings which constrain him to come to terms with them. The preceding chapter has emphasized the first, the original aspect of the situation—namely, the fact of the confrontation. The present chapter focuses attention upon the second or corollary aspect, that of man's response to the realities which break in upon him. The immediate question is whether or not varying degrees of response fully account for the vicissitudes of revelation in the wider acceptation of the term.

It stands to reason that just as there would be no knowledge without the confrontation just characterized, the resulting disclosure would remain a dead letter apart from some kind of reaction to it. Our knowledge is of events, that is, of entities constituted by both disclosure and response. History for example consists of happenings together with the meaning or meanings ascribed to them. Had there been no kind of response whatsoever to this or that happening, it would not be part of history. History implies selection because it involves interpretation. Thus we must go to the evangelists to secure information about Jesus. He was not "history" for the secular historians of his day. (The authoritative *Cambridge Modern History*, although a monumental work, finds room for only one single mention of the word "missionary." Yet the reference is to Missionary Ridge in Tennessee where a skirmish took place during the Civil War. But why labor the point?) The news which makes headlines every morning should remind us if need be that history does not mean the same thing to different people. A historical event in the last analysis is existence actualized for better or for worse in terms of response.

How then can we account for the fact that in a given situation there are irresponsive or partly responsive people? In some cases personal and social limitations may be involved. Thus the Egyptologist H. Kees has drawn attention to the connection of the tomb autobiographies of two noblemen who lived under Sesostris I one generation after 2000 B.C. Both these men responded to the fact that wealth had come to them by dealing righteously in the dispensation of justice.[1] Quite a limited degree of response, and a response of debatable quality at that! In the steellike coldness of a cynic on the other hand, there is either no evidence of a response at all or there is a response to an alien motivation. The ease with which Queen Elizabeth I as portrayed by J. R. Greene asserted or denied whatever suited her purpose is said to have been equaled only by the cynical indifference with which she met the exposure of her lies. Here the impression is that of a blank or a blind spot in a human conscience. But then think of Peter when the cock crowed and the Lord turned around and looked at him. "And he went outside and wept bitterly." We know what Peter's ultimate response finally turned out to be. Truly the gist of all genuine response—and this again for better or for worse—is summed up in the proposition already stated, "I respond, although I shall be changed," possibly accounting for the fact that some hesitate to respond. They are simply not ready to pay the price.

A failure to respond, or to respond fully because of blindness or fear of the cost, may account for our shortcomings. Let no Pharisaism single out modernity for an indictment at this juncture. Surely coldness and loss of radiance in a Christian expose his profession as a sham. Similarly, a reluctance to welcome fresh information for fear of losing a false peace betrays a lack of readiness to pay the cost. And so even in their weaknesses both Christianity and modernity testify to a basic similitude with regard to whatever degree of revelation has come to them.

Possibly the most striking conclusion reached thus far in this chapter is that response involves change. But what kind of change? Because of the truly "eventful" character of the knowing process, it would seem that the knower is in a real way changed into that which he comes to know. Or perhaps we should say that as far as may be observed, he henceforth exhibits features characteristic of the known which affects him. This, incidentally, is the reason we should attend to the kind of company we keep. Influence is "influx," literally "flowing into," whether in terms of motive, ability, or quality. In a phrase like "the influence of example," the word "influence" points to the property or process of producing modifications. To all practical purposes, response at this point is one and the same as change. The reason the devotional classic *Imitation of Christ* never loses its potency is that in this special case the imitation is that of One who can change the reader of goodwill to a degree otherwise unknown to mortal man. What has just been said of *Imitation of Christ* applies infinitely more to a meditation upon the Gospel. Ruminating upon the Gospel story in simplicity of heart constitutes a truly sacramental activity because the features of the picture conveyed are "charged" with the living God. This is why Christ could use such a figure as "feeding upon" him. This is also why he is the great healer, for to heal is also to change, to restore to health that which was sick.

To respond is indeed to be changed. Hence the degree of response is also the degree of the capacity to be changed which we call "addressability." Professor Charles Hartshorne has coined the happy phrase "sympathetic dependence" to convey the same meaning. He has illustrated it by suggesting the following mental experiment:

> Imagine someone to read aloud an eloquent poem, in the presence of: (A) a glass of water, (B) an ant, (C) a dog, (D) a human being unacquainted with the language of the poem, (E) a human being knowing the language but insensitive to poetry, (F) a person sensitive to poetry and familiar with the language. Now I submit that each member of this series is superior, in terms of the data, to its predecessors, and that each is more, not less, dependent upon or relative to the poem as such, including its meanings as well as its mere sounds. The molecule of water will be utterly "impassible" (the theological term) to the words of the poem as words, and not even much affected by the mere physical sounds. The ant, since it has hearing, will be affected by the physical sounds more drastically, it seems probable, than the water. The dog will not only hear and be influenced by the sound, as such, but will have some sense of the emotional tones of the voice, and may be quite excited by these. It may also have a feeling of familiarity concerning some of the words. The human being not knowing the language will receive more varied influences of this kind and will enjoy some sense of the verbal music of the poem, which may furnish a rather absorbing experience. The insensitive, but comprehending, listener will be given a variety of images and ideas, even though without intense esthetic feeling or adequate integration. The adequate listener may go through a deep and thousandfold adventure of thought and feeling.[2]

Professor Hartshorne's experiment would likely be pronounced preposterous, were he to limit his comparison to the two extreme terms. While everybody would follow him when he spoke of reading an eloquent poem to a person sensitive to poetry and familiar with the language, real anxiety with regard to his mental health would likely follow upon his suggestion of reading the poem to a glass of water. And yet in each instance a basic analogy would testify to the relevance of the illustration. This relevance, however, only comes within view once the intervening terms are set up in their gradualness—namely, the case of the ant, that of the dog, and those of the human beings concerned.

The reason radical theologians establish a dichotomy between a man's response to God and a man's response to any kind of reality which impinges upon him is that the distance between the two is so great as to hide whatever similitude there may be. And this amounts to defeatism. I am afraid that the theologian who once assured me that Socrates never knew God was a victim of the error of perspective to which reference has just been made. Only the vastness of the difference which separates two events with regard to their likely proximity to God can so blind the observer that he will isolate one from the other. To the radical theologian of the Word, the response of a Luther to the free and sovereign grace of God does not seem to have any relation whatsoever to the response of Socrates in the death scene evoked in Plato's *Phaedo.* What would it be, one may wonder, were we to use as another illustration of response the reaction of Captain Peleg in Melville's *Moby Dick,* when he saw Quequeg's harpoon strike the glistening tar spot out of sight.[3] His utilitarian reaction amounts to near impassibility in the theological acceptation of the term. Little does Captain Peleg realize during this hiring session that what is at stake in Ahab's obsessive desire for vengeance on Moby Dick is nothing short of an assault upon "all that most maddens and torments; all that stirs up the lees of things; all truth with malice in it; all that cracks the sinews and cakes the brain; all the subtle demonisms of life and thought; all evil. . . ."[4] And so the elemental response of Captain Peleg misses most of the wider context of the undertaking in which he participates.

Heeding the relevance of the pointer previously provided in the mental experiment suggested by Professor Hartshorne, let us now gradually proceed from the elemental response of Captain Peleg to instances likely to bring us ever closer to more adequate types of response. Let us take up the case of a man whose very name is still anathema to many an evangelical Christian—Charles Darwin.

As he came to the end of his epoch-making work, *The Origin of Species,* Charles Darwin witnessed to the conviction that had been forced upon his intellectual honesty by inescapable facts and considerations—namely, that species have actually been modified during a long course of existence. As he summarized his findings in his final section, "Recapitulation and Conclusion," he insisted that he saw no good reason why these same findings "should shock the religious feelings of anyone." To him there was a grandeur in a view of life traced back to several powers "originally breathed by the Creator into a few forms or into one." What had ultimately been disclosed to him as he responded to it was a more accurate understanding of the ways of God. And yet Darwin might be the first to admit that whatever the aftermath of his encounter with the realities of creation may have been, he would not think of comparing the transforming influence of that encounter to that of an immediate confrontation with the living Christ. Nevertheless, restricted as it was, the revelation which came to Darwin must in good faith be pronounced genuine.

And now reaching for a higher level of disclosure, as it were, let us recall the case of Albert Schweitzer, to which reference has already been made. It is current practice to pay tribute to the humanitarianism of the good doctor while suggesting that his basic principle of Reverence for Life has little to do with the Gospel. Yet I submit that this view cannot possibly have taken into account such evidence as is available in *The Mystery of the Kingdom of God,* the last seventy pages of *The Quest of the Historical Jesus,* the whole of his magnificent *The Mysticism of Paul the Apostle,* and the epilogue of *My Life and Thought* further brought up to date in the epilogue Schweitzer wrote for Mozley's little book *The Theology of Albert Schweitzer for Christian Inquirers.* The man of Lambaréné makes it clear, both in text and context, that to him the ethic of Reverence for Life is in essence the ethic of Jesus, inasmuch as all spiritual life meets us within natural life. With a gentle sense of humor, Schweitzer further draws attention to the fact that "in the parable of Jesus, the shepherd saves not merely the soul of the lost sheep but the whole animal."[5]

The point of the newly formulated principle of Reverence for Life is that henceforth the ethic of Jesus may be acknowledged as a logical consequence of thought. This, together with the fact that it universalizes the ethic of love, makes it truly final. If it were not so the trivial qualification of "emotional" might once more dispose of the heavenly beauty inherent in the illustration. Or disquisition with regard to scales of values might initiate processes of grave hairsplitting. What is new in the principle of Schweitzer, what makes it truly invaluable, is that it legitimates the omission of all distinction between higher value and lower value, between more and less valuable life. And how is this done? Essentially by exposing once for all the anthropocentric character of the current distinctions. *We* postulate these scales of values. *We* establish between living beings greater or lesser distances according to our own empirical, subjective criterion. And yet who among us would honestly claim to know the real significance which this or that form of life has in itself, as a part of the work of creation? Only the Creator knows, and it is his criterion which strikes us in the parable of Jesus. But, some may further object, did not Schweitzer close his *Quest* with the evocation of Jesus coming to us "as One unknown, without a name, as of old, by the lakeside, He came to those men who knew Him not"?[6] Yes, Schweitzer used these words. Before we take him to task, however, we had better make sure that we actually know this same Jesus, whom those by the lakeside knew not. We had better make sure above all that we actually know this Jesus better than Albert Schweitzer does.

How then did Albert Schweitzer come to know Jesus? There was to be sure the amazing amount of labor that went into the epoch-making *Quest,* to name only the most important title here under consideration. Yet the fact remains that other scholars have devoted a similar amount of labor to the same quest and may hardly be said to have found Jesus, or better, to have been found by Jesus in the way Schweitzer has been found. And this is a great mystery. Yet a mystery is not utter darkness. Mystery is a luminous center which grows in ardor as one dwells on it. A mystery is an invitation to pilgrimage. What forces attention in the case of Schweitzer is that his response rose in intensity as the encounter with Jesus became more and more pressing and insistent. And so it was that the phrase "Reverence for Life" suddenly flashed "unforeseen and unsought" upon his whole being.[7] Lo and behold, Jesus was the very heart of it. Schweitzer's response, then, must be pronounced a full response, the final consummation of a change which had come to him through decades of obedience to the light he had.

Whatever its fullness, however, the response of an Albert Schweitzer still remains in part a mediated response. For a truly immediate and total response we must proceed higher still. Here is Saul the hater and persecutor of Christians on his way to Damascus to "bind those who had gathered there and bring them back to Jerusalem for punishment." As he nears his destination at the noon hour, suddenly a brilliant heavenly light flashes round him. He drops to the earth and hears a voice saying to him, "Saul, Saul, why do you persecute me?" "Who are you?" he asks. The Other says to him, "I am Jesus," and he entrusts him with a divine Purpose. We know that Saul was not disobedient to the heavenly vision. His response was a total response. Therefore it involved a total change amounting to transfiguration. His whole life was revolutionized in the process. His religious objectives were redefined. The prosecutor of Christianity was turned into its most ardent promoter. His Jewish theology was utterly reconstructed in the light which had blinded him on the road to Damascus. It became the very prototype of the theology of the Body of Christ.

How well we understand at this apex those children of light who want no part in infinitely lesser versions of revelation! They remind one of an Augustine well on his way to Christian service, stating that he no longer found pleasure in reading pagan books because the name of Jesus was not in them.

Such an attitude, however, does not do justice to the deeper realities of the case, as the preceding considerations must have shown by now. Accordingly it is unwise, not to say, uncalled for. It amounts to a sin against what the old British Fabian socialists called "the inevitability of gradualness." By this phrase, incidentally, they meant to convey the bitterness likely to be engendered by too hasty a transition. The danger involved in the situation, as they saw it, was that undue precipitation might cancel out the advances already secured. Yet there is for us Christians infinitely more at stake than a wise policy, more even than a readiness to heed the Master's admonition to be "wise as serpents." "The inevitability of gradualness" in the context of the present chapter would appear to pertain to the very economy of this created world. As such it would seem to be destined, in Bacon's words, to lead "from a study of the created works to a contemplation of the Creator."

Shall we conclude, then, that the reason a man does not gain access to the higher revelation, which is God himself in his saving Act in Christ, is to be detected in too low a level of response? That as a result the sense of the basic unity of all existence is lost together with an inherent sense of the true purpose of life? If it be so, and if what ultimately matters is the total response of the whole man to the totality of apprehended reality, then the unity of science and of the Faith is at hand for all men of goodwill. But there are difficulties.

Before we consider these difficulties, however, we should gratefully acknowledge the precious character of the elements of certitude which have come to us thus far. None of the forthcoming reservations may detract from the gratification we feel at the thought that a greater receptivity and response on our part to whatever truth breaks in upon us is bound to be rewarded a thousandfold. Also that the certification of the human mind will come within our common reach to the degree to which we share the insights gained through a more hearty openness. To be sure these same insights will be subject to discussion and correction on the part of every relevant science concerned the moment they are found to involve any specific human context. For instance, historical events in and through which an insight is conveyed remain at all times open to the scrutiny of source criticism, as well as to that of the psychological, social, and historical disciplines, the autonomy of each and the categories it sees fit to use being taken for granted. It stands to reason, however, that the ultimate validity of the insights which constitute this or that particular disclosure can neither be vindicated nor threatened thereby. And now for some essential reservations.

I need hardly insist that the Christian way out of man's plight is not essentially the way of knowledge, however important that may prove to be. Redemption from ignorance, in fact, finds little commendation in the Bible. Neither need I insist that the nearer the events involved in knowledge lie to God and to the things of God, the more the converse knowledge is likely to be affected by man's relative estrangement from God. Emil Brunner, it will be remembered, has pointed out to us that while the disturbance under consideration reaches its minimum in the exact sciences and becomes insignificant in the realm of the formal, it increases through the human sciences to reach its maximum in theology.

The point is constantly verified in the realm of factual realities. It will call for closer consideration in the coming chapters. But this much has already become clear—namely, that the traditional way of ascribing the divergence at hand to a cleavage between modernity and Christianity is both superficial and irrelevant.

In spite of the great possibilities inherent in a more spontaneous, more widely open response to the realities which break in upon us, revelation in its wider meaning remains largely conditioned by divergent basic attitudes. Our next task, then, is to try to discover what these attitudes actually are.

PART IV

The Promethean Character of
A Common Plight

13

Cutting Across Established Views

A. with reference to the classical view of *hamartia*

ONE OF the most deeply entrenched views in theology today is that the plight of Christian thinking through the ages must be ascribed to the adaptation of our Western culture to Greek ways of understanding. And the verb "to adapt" is often too close for comfort to the verb "to adopt." In a lecture delivered at the University of Cambridge J. S. Whale put the matter in a nutshell with the curt statement that "if Greek thought creates a difficulty for religion, Hebrew religion creates a difficulty for thought."[1] What I am about to suggest—and in so doing I am aware that I shall be going against the grain—is that this well-worn study in contrast of Hebrew versus Greek may no longer be telling the whole story.

I hope to convince the reader that the basic attitudes to be dealt with in this chapter and the next afford a contrast in different terms. In other words, the great divide which I shall attempt to map out afresh no longer delineates the same areas the traditional cleavage did, especially with respect to the crucial issue of sin. It was this issue which finally frustrated our attempt to account for revelation solely in terms of variations in degrees of response. It has always been so whenever men have earnestly tried to bring modernity and Christianity closer together in order to secure for both the certification of the human mind. I would therefore beg leave to bring into the open this irritating question of the disturbance brought about by sin in the process of knowledge. The time has come to face it since it is now the stumbling block right across our path.

Once a Christian student has recovered a sufficient degree of independence of mind and cut loose from deeply set, well-established traditional solutions, he may hope to get access to fresh information. The trouble with any kind of fresh information, however, is that it is bound to prove disturbing, at least at the outset. I have already pointed out that our first impression whenever we learn anything new is that we have lost something.

The first impression likely to disturb us in the present case—only to prove enlightening once we have taken a straight look at it—is that the notion of sin, far from being a biblical monopoly, is deeply embedded in our classical heritage.

The same word *hamartia* which constitutes the essential connotation of sin in the New Testament runs through classical Greek use. Its connotation there lies at the core of Greek tragedy to the point of becoming the animating principle of it. As such it stands for "mistake," "mistaken way," hence for "missing the mark." This last ascription also happens to be an essential one in the Gospels and the Epistles. Yet, as we shall shortly realize, their common feature may prove misleading. The term *hamartia* in its classical use applies to some kind of shortcoming certain to exact painful retribution, more exactly to an inward flaw which of necessity originates the fatal error. This, for example, is the case with King Oedipus whose blind, impulsive rashness plays into the hands of fate. Sophocles provides another illustration of the same meaning in *Antigone* as Creon ascribes the unleashing of endless woes upon his household to

> my purblind wisdom's fatal guilt
> Stubborn, and fraught with death!

Alas for him, the benevolent Chorus can only express regret at his having been too late in discerning the truth. A suggestion of possible salvation through the Greek way of knowledge, that is, redemption from ignorance, seems to put in an appearance here. But the impression is misleading. The fault in Creon's wisdom is referred to by Sophocles as a "fatal guilt." The pertinent suggestion, therefore, is rather that of necessity, of unavoidable sequence. The principle of necessity in Greek tragedy is conveyed by the plot (*muthos*). And it is noteworthy that according to the *Poetics* of Aristotle, the whole structure is an imitation of an action that is serious, complete in itself, and of an adequate magnitude. Hence the tragic effect wrought out by the menacing attitudes of the Furies in *The Eumenides,* or by the wretched, starved appearance of Sophocles' Electra, whose father's eye

> Saw death advancing from the ruthless pair,
> Conjoint in cruel villainy,
> By whom my life was plunged in black despair . . .

How could Electra bear it?

It is because of this element of necessity conveyed by the plot that disclosure becomes so tragic, according to the principle of recognition (*anagnorisis*). Indeed this recognition grows out of the very nature of things. While it may once more appear as a promise of redemption through knowledge, the opposite is the case. It is actually a revelation which reaches the marked man on schedule, and the schedule is a tragic one. It is a schedule of doom. A climax of terror is reached when murderers and victims recognize each other, as when Clytemnestra kills her husband in the *Agamemnon* of Aeschylus. So also when Orestes kills his mother and her newly wedded husband, Orestes' blood-foe, in Aeschylus'

Choëphoroe. Since it is the climax which brings the whole matter to a head, I quote the ultimate exchange of words between Orestes and his mother:

> "Yea, from the grave my father speaks thy doom."
> "Ah God! The serpent that I bare and fed!"
> "Surely of truth prophetic is the dread
> That walketh among dreams. Most sinfully
> Thou slewest: now hath Sin her will of thee."

The very consistency of the entire event is grounded in the fatal character of necessity operating through mortals whose own nature cannot change because it pertains to the very nature of things. Even their way of arguing (*dianoia*), that is, their power to say what suits a given situation, belongs in the same tragic picture. And so the dramatization finally amounts to a rationalization. Already the tragic view may be identified as typically anthropocentric. We are now well on our way to a further characterization of anthropomorphism, a notion which may be said to have plagued us throughout this inquiry.

The keen Bible student is sure to have realized already how far apart from the Christian understanding of sin this tragic view of sin as *hamartia* actually is. The genuinely prophetic and Christian notion of sin is essentially that of alienation from an all-loving God who truly grieves over an estrangement amounting to betrayal. This grief comes out in the words of Jeremiah, "They have forsaken me;" better still, in the Parable of the Prodigal Son. Its reference is to the attitude adopted by the whole man. This is why sin in its Christian acceptation may be said to be a singular of which there is no plural.

Yet my chief concern at this point is not with a contrast between the tragic view and the Christian view *per se*. It is with the degree to which current evangelical views have been contaminated by the tragic view, with the result that the subsequent dividing line is found to cut across the traditional cleavage, Greek versus Hebrew-Christian.

The suggestion of this or that kind of tragic flaw has resulted in a generalized use of sin in the plural, whether or not an impressive biblical singular was meant. Even that basic disloyalty the Scripture calls sin has been turned into sins. First into a hierarchy of sins grounded in a distinction between mortal sin and venial sin. Then into a variety of sins singled out as capital sins, viz., pride, covetousness, lust, anger, gluttony, envy, sloth. Sinners have accordingly been advised to eradicate these flaws one by one as the case may be. A proper analogy for the practice is provided by Benjamin Franklin, who followed his moral progress by evaluating it in terms of the decreasing number of black marks he put down to his debit in his diary. This kind of procedure may be good practice in the context of the *Nicomachean Ethics* of Aristotle, the ideal man becoming the implementation of the tragic hero of the *Poetics*. But it is hardly a Christian view.

We come next to the *sui generis* element of fatal necessity inherent in the tragic view of sin as *hamartia*. It obviously has no room for the redeeming grace of God. Rather it leaves man to the sheer determinism of the nature of things moving on their own accord. This applies to the status of man apart from the totalitarian state, according to Hobbes' *Leviathan*. Once more the stage is set for Eugene O'Neill's *Long Day's Journey Into Night*.

There is above all an overemphasis on the *fatal* character of original sin understood as a *personal* guilt unavoidably inherited, together with its ominous implications. As if I had sinned in Adam, not as what I am, but as who I am! And there are those crude theories of atonement seemingly devised by Origen and brought into full expression by Anselm, according to which, only a blood ransom duly paid to God, conceived as a feudal overlord,

[129]

can possibly break up the fatal determinism. We are again confronted with a tragic view which amounts to anthropomorphism. To all practical purposes the saving power of the Cross of Christ has been reduced to theoretical concepts accessible to our human infirmity and likely to betray their human origination. I need not insist that these anthropomorphic views go a long way in alienating modernity.

Probably the strangest "Christian" counterpart of the tragic notion of sin as fatal error appears in the liturgical phrase *felix culpa,* "fortunate guilt," which points to the fall of Adam. Even Milton appropriated this notion in the Twelfth Book of *Paradise Lost.* The gist of this use of *felix culpa* is that the fall brought about the need for redemption. Had Adam not transgressed, we should not have had the second Adam, even our Lord Jesus Christ.[2] Or should we? What is the ground for this one-way necessity wherein man dramatizes his version of sacred history? Milton incidentally found it advisable to limit the creative power of God. The reason his God is presented as contending with Chaos in *Paradise Lost* is that he allegedly could not have created this world out of nothing. What he then chose to do, according to Milton, was to shape things out of a formless, pre-existent matter. Such a God, I suggest, looks more like the artificer or demiurge Plato introduces in the half-mythological *Timaeus,* than like the Creator presented in the opening verse of the Book of Genesis. The only noticeable difference is that, while in Plato the sensible world merely receives its intelligibility from one who keeps his eyes fixed upon the Ideas, Milton's God uses matter which has proceeded out of him somewhere in time. In all fairness to the author of *Paradise Lost,* it should be made clear that this, like many of his other heterodoxies,[3] had its origin in his own exegesis of the Bible as evidenced in *De Doctrina Christiana,* Milton's private confession of faith. The truth of the matter is that a failure to take into account this admittedly obscure title has been responsible for a great many misgivings on the part of Milton's critics.

So much then for the classical view of sin as *hamartia*. Otherwise the classical view of sin in its most tragic aspects can only yield its fuller implications once its wider conditioning has been taken into consideration, a conditioning of mighty opposites contrasted to the point of absolute otherness. And lo and behold, we are beginning to talk like the Karl Barth of his Kierkegaardian period. That this is no mere chance happening will readily appear in the following chapter where a second, still more virulent classical view of sin will come under consideration—namely, the classical view of sin as *hubris*.

14

Cutting Across Established Views (Continued)

B. with reference to the classical view of *hubris*

THE tragic view of mighty opposites goes back to time immemorial. For the sake of brevity, however, and in order to keep this chapter within reasonable bounds, I shall be satisfied to illustrate some of its early aspects.

In the *Theogony* of Hesiod (eighth century B.C.), we are confronted by the vision of gods born of Earth and Sky in the midst of Chaos, when the starry heaven was loosened from its earthly embrace. In a similar vein, the sixth century B.C. Chinese philosopher Lao-tse, the founder of Taoism, ascribed the origin of all life to the clash of Tao's manifestations, Yang (the positive process) and Yin (the negative) conceived as counterparts. This type of dramatization is further found in Heracleitus and the Eleatics. The Sophists made the most of this setup in their dialectics. Plato had the same kind of polarity in mind in the famous passage of his *Phaedrus* in which the human soul is likened to a chariot drawn by two horses, one pulling up, and the other down. And so Ovid: "Desire counsels me in one direction, reason in another"; "I see and approve the better, but I follow the worse." Following upon this disjunction, sin is apprehended as inherent in dramatized forms of conflict. Says Epictetus, "He who sins does not what he would, and does what he would not." And again Seneca: "What, then, is it that, when we would go in one direction, drags us in the other?" Incidentally, the conservative Swiss commentator Frederick Godet has identified in this context Rom. 7:23 as the verse in all the epistles of Paul which presents the most points of contact with classical literature: "But I see another law in my members, warring against the law of my mind, and bringing me into captivity to the law of sin which is in my members."

The stage is now set for a consideration of the view of sin by far the most characteristic in tragedy, that of *hubris*. The meaning of the word is not adequately conveyed in the current translation "pride." The reference is rather to people who are misled by wanting too much, even daring the impossible, and this ultimately out of pride. Their arrogant, intemperate ways are bound to bring down upon them the wrath of Zeus through the retribution of Nemesis. Once *hubris* has affected them, Ate, the goddess of infatuation, assails and blinds them. No wonder Creon in *Antigone* could not understand in time what was in the nature of things!

The sin of *hubris* constitutes the leading theme of Greek tragedy just as obsession with it dominates Greek life and mythology. The fact that the fable or plot (*muthos*) represents in the drama the action which the author imitates, constitutes the plot as the first principle, the very soul of tragedy. Thus in the historical drama *The Persians*, Xerxes is guilty of this sin of *hubris* for having challenged the gods who had set the waters of the Hellespont to divide Asia from Europe. The classical illustration of *hubris*, however, remains Prometheus, the great challenger of Zeus. In *Prometheus Bound*, Aeschylus dramatizes the myth. Zeus has defeated the Titans with the aid of Prometheus (Forethought), who had previously deserted their ranks. His supremacy over the universe once established however, Zeus has become despotic. He has ultimately decided to destroy men and to replace them by a better race. Defying his decrees, Prometheus steals forbidden fire and brings it down from heaven to mortals, together with the heavenly secrets of arts and crafts which he has snatched away in order to better the lot of mankind. This is the essence of *hubris,* namely, a defiant transgression for the sake of some self-appointed achievement which may prove praiseworthy, yet is sure to release calamity—all in all a suicidal aspiration. In arrogating to himself the prerogatives of Zeus, even for laudable motives, the heaven-storming hero has called down upon himself a wrathful, divine retribution. The most vivid presentation of the sin of *hubris* flashes upon us when, at the height of this daring defiance, Zeus unleashes a terrific storm. The rock to which Prometheus had been bound is struck by lightning, and the earth gapes wide open to engulf the challenger of heaven.

There comes to light a radical ambiguity in the double perspective of *hubris,* in that the proud egocentricity of the sinner constitutes the full measure of his sin, the nobility of his motives notwithstanding. Hence a tragic element, in that, viewed from a purely human vantage point, the transgression is seen to have been animated by a virtue. Here again, and more than ever, the tragic view betrays its thoroughly anthropocentric character. Prometheus is the prototype of the independent, self-affirming life of flesh and blood at its best. He has his offspring in the noblest strivings of a modernity which chooses to proceed on its own whatever the cost. Modern man is essentially hybridic, Promethean; it is both his nobility and his doom. In a universally human context, therefore, *hubris* is not to be characterized as a Greek version of sin, but rather as the tragic view of sin.

In *The Golden Bough,* James G. Frazer has noted a radical conflict between magic and religion. His striking presentation amounts to a transposition of the sin of *hubris,* as the truly Promethean magician contends with the reverent man of God. As Frazer sees it, the haughty self-sufficiency of the magician, his arrogant demeanor toward the higher powers, and his unabashed claim to exercise a sway like theirs, cannot but revolt the priest. The priest, on the other hand, is moved to reverence by an awful sense of the divine majesty. This is why he apprehends as impious and blasphemous, the claims and demeanor of a challenger bent upon usurping prerogatives that belong to God alone. Accordingly,. while the normal attitude of the priest is that of a man of prayer on his knees, the normal attitude of the magician is that of an arrogant man arising in defiance.

We find in these considerations the explanation of the anathema confounding alchemists with sorcerers. Even the science of nature has appeared to be an independent personality intervening in the course of beings and things created and governed by God. The alchemist also is an impatient one who, like Faust, gives himself up to magic in his haste to reach his goal. What matter the means along this ascending line, provided one succeed in tapping the unknown powers which produce phenomena, and in making them act in accordance with one's will?

Therefore to magic I gave myself up.

Or think of the priest Claude Frollo in Victor Hugo's *The Hunchback of Notre Dame.* This ecclesiastic is known as an alchemist. He is one of those men who play fast and loose with the powers of mystery, and no one ever succeeds in that sort of business unless he is ready to sell his soul, which is a particularly serious matter for a priest. Having exhausted the *fas* of human knowledge, he has dared penetrate into the *nefas* in a truly Promethean quest. His learned and impassioned imagination delights in fathoming the cathedral's secrets, in deciphering the scat-

[135]

tered symbols of its sculptures, in a word, in solving the enigma which it eternally proposes to the inquiring mind. In one of the towers he has furnished a mysterious den where strange lights burn at night. "There is the archdeacon blowing his bellow," say the old women from down below on the square.

There are good reasons to identify magicians and alchemists as the ancestors of the scientist as we know him today. And who would deny for one moment that many of us still look at the latter very much in the way our medieval forefathers beheld his predecessors? The prototype is there, and it is a Promethean prototype. The "sin" of the scientist remains that of Prometheus— namely, the tragic sin of *hubris*. He does not submit to mystery. He challenges it. He searches for knowledge because he wants power. With haughty presumption he does not hesitate to snatch the power of the atom or even to create an earth satellite, heretofore a divine prerogative. The reason we have just been confronted by these biblical versions of the sin of *hubris* is that we have by now reached far into a Christianized Western civilization. In this situation, as was previously the case for the original forms of *hubris,* the new versions can yield their fuller implications only in the context of mighty opposites.

The double perspective in the Hebrew-Christian tradition has arisen from the constitution of a world of Darkness conceived of as the counterpart of the world of Light. The world of Darkness is the realm of Satan. The world of Light is the realm of God the Creator.

Clearly, there should be no such cleavage. While the Scriptures present Satan as standing in opposition to God, they introduce him as a creature, not as an uncreated existence on a par with the Eternal. One of the sons of God, he is further said to have been entrusted with special functions, assigned certain obligations. His power has been strictly limited, and in the end he is definitely subject to the divine will.

There can be no question of mighty opposites here, and all the more so as "the Lord is gracious, and full of compassion; slow to anger, and of great mercy. The Lord is good to all: and his tender mercies are over all his works." Accordingly, he is "the great Doer of redeeming things," not willing that any of the sons of men should perish, but rather that they should have life, and have it abundantly. He is above all the father of our Lord Jesus Christ. "The Word was made flesh and dwelt among us." "God so loved the world, that he gave his only begotten Son, that whosoever believeth in him should not perish, but have everlasting life." This is the prophetic view, the truly evangelical view.

In this light then, as we look at sin from the side of God, and conversely from that of the Evil One, we find the tragic tension reduced to a point where the very notion of mighty opposites becomes inadequate to account for the situation. Accordingly, the climate which we formerly associated with *hubris* has radically changed. The whole burden of the Bible, in fact, is that our deliverance is from the tragic view which spells necessity, doom, and despair. We are admonished by the Lord of the vineyard to come in, even at this eleventh hour. Not because the Lord of the vineyard plays favorites, but because he is good.

Indeed, this is no longer the anthropocentric, tragic view; it is a God-given prophetic view we could never have devised on our own. Professor Edmond LaB. Cherbonnier has a delightfully penetrating way of suggesting the kind of world it involves. While questioning the historicity of the Old Testament account of God's walking on the earth in the cool of the day, he remarks that God is, nevertheless, the kind of God who could do so if he chose.[1] Again there is deep truth in the ladder which dreaming Jacob saw set up on earth and reaching to heaven, with the angels

of God ascending and descending on it. Yet infinitely more edifying still is our Lord's prayer that the will of God be done on
earth, as it is in heaven. All the *sine qua non* conditions which
used to originate the Promethean double perspective of *hubris* thus
fade away under the blinding sun of the Gospel on this hallowed
hillside. The prophetic view simply negates the tragic view.

Alas, we have been speaking of what ought to be, if the Bible
were rightly understood. The tragic view with its sin of *hubris*
and its double perspective still thrives in our midst, essentially because the proper breeding ground for it has been provided.

In an age of repressive morality, the medieval Church was insistent upon the horrible character of Hell, the counterpart of
Paradise. In this frame of mind it was actually preparing in the
imaginations of the people the conception of a kingdom whose
throne could be properly occupied by Satan. The devil thus en-
throned rallied to his standard the baleful creatures who were
without leadership. Hitherto the world of witchcraft had remained
amorphous, lacking an organizing principle. Oddly enough, it was
for the Church and for heresies to bring to the world of witchcraft,
elements which would put an end to chaos.

Accordingly, the witches issued from their obscurity and took
their places in a new society which was opposed to that of the
children of God. And so Satan was seen gliding in as the fires of
Hell began to burn afresh, and he found legions of sorcerers ready
to understand him. His very existence became an article of faith.
Architecture, in default of a book which would have been in-
decipherable to the vulgar, popularized the effigy of the Prince of
Darkness. Gutters, gargoyles, spandrels of the portals, and furni-
ture of the vestry presented with terrible realism the devil, his
acolytes, a frightful last judgment, and the gulf of Hell teeming
with torments.

The literature of that age seems to have delighted in atrocious pictures of Hell. The religious theater of the Middle Ages represents Hell as dragon jaws, lighted by flames and belching smoke. From underground issue the moanings of the damned and the howlings of the demons. When, in the *Divine Comedy,* Dante descends into the funnel with the nine steps, he progresses toward ever greater horrors. And at the very bottom the Other—Lucifer:

> How great a marvel it did seem to me
> When to that head three faces I beheld!
> One was before, and it was purplish red;
> Whilst the two other faces, both conjoined
> Above each shoulder's middle with the first,
> Were at the crest united, each to each;
> The right face seemed of hue 'twixt white and yellow;
> The left was swarth like men of Aethiope's soil;
> Outward from either one, spread two broad wings,
> In form and sweep befitting such a bird:—
> No ocean craft ever bore sails so huge—.
> The wings were featherless like wings of bats,
> And from the three there issued forth three winds,
> Congealing with their blasts that gulf of tears;
> And from six eyes he wept, and down three chins
> He dribbled forth his plaints and bloody foam,
> His teeth craunching a sinner in each maw,
> Like brakes crushing the fibre of crude flax;
> Yet being ground by teeth as nothing seemed
> To him i' the hither maw, for two fierce claws
> Ever rent bare his flesh from off his spine.[2]

Henceforth a world of Darkness has been fully constituted as a mighty counterpart to the world of Light—the perfect setting for a Christian version of *hubris.* Luther had to struggle hard to free himself from its terrors. We are told that his struggle culminated in the reformer's throwing his inkstand into the face of the great

Rival, who indeed seems not to have been killed on the spot as a humorist has claimed.

It was especially in order to protect itself against any possible surprise that Roman Catholic piety provided rosaries and a multiplicity of medals. It was in order to deliver those possessed by Satan and his stooges that this same Catholic piety provided the ceremony of exorcism. For a long time terrifying and complicated, the ceremony was subsequently reduced in the ritual to prayer and exhortation. Yet this built-in picture of a kingdom of Darkness existing on a par with the kingdom of Light has lingered in the popular imagination down to our day, even in the Reformed tradition. It is indeed not rare to hear the question, "Do you believe in the devil?" raised with the same earnestness as the other question, "Do you accept Jesus Christ as your personal savior?" As if the implications of the second question do not utterly contradict the built-in, fatal implications of the first! The next chapters will make it clear that this critique does not constitute my last word on the subject. Our Lord himself took the issue of evil too seriously for that. Be it sufficient to say in the light of our previous conclusions that a first fruitful way to approach the problem would be to divest it of its pseudo-aspects, beginning with its tragic Promethean features.

We may further cut across established views, by realizing that a current insistence on sin as essentially pride must be pronounced a Christianized version of the tragic view of *hubris*. And so, above all, is the enormous amount of false humility which prides itself at not being proud, with the result that a man may become obsessed with his own self-centeredness. Guilt complexes soon are likely to be upon him, as he increasingly loses touch with the divine simplicity of the Gospel. In one case which came to my attention a young Christian actually took his life.

At a more exalted level we come to grips with a still more

virulent version of Christianized *hubris*—namely, that of the existential proclamation of the wholly-Otherness of God. It was Kierkegaard, as far as I know, who revived the dictum, *finitum non capax infiniti* (the finite cannot bear the infinite), currently credited to Karl Barth. The truth is that Karl Barth seized upon it during his existential period to provide a structure for his Calvinism in revolt.

And yet the plain fact is that *finitum non capax infiniti* has long been the tragic expression of the dilemma Prometheus owed to his double perspective. As such it continues to be the motto of a fateful dramatization, the clearest outcome of which is the re-establishment of "mighty" opposites—in this case, a Promethean natural man in revolt (*Widerspruch*) against God. This new Lucifer (*Lichtträger*) hurls defiance at an utterly inaccessible Other over the unbridgeable chasm which spells total alienation. In view of his plight, natural man well might use the profession of faith Goethe puts into the mouth of Mephistopheles in his *Faust*,

> *Ich bin der Geist, der stets verneint . . .*
> (I am the spirit who chooses to deny . . .)

Such a radical theological tenet is likely to call forth the Prometheus slumbering in every man of flesh and blood. To say that the finite is best instructed by the infinite is one thing. To assert that there is in the finite nothing that prepares it to approach the infinite is quite another thing, in fact, a terrible thing.

Karl Barth has now seen this. I have had occasion to emphasize his rupture with the Kierkegaardian, existential approach, his providential rediscovery of Anselm, then his subsequent shift from the wholly-Otherness of God to a lofty view of God's sovereign free grace. And so the nightmare should be over. Or is it?

The tragic view still looms large in Christian circles today.

Christianized versions of Prometheus come to life again and again in our day and age because a resurgence of the double perspective, from different angles and in varying contexts, makes it essentially a tragic age. I think of men like Freud, Sartre, Faulkner, Bernanos, and Kafka, to name only a few at random.

There seems, alas, to be a law according to which public and especially Christian instruction lags behind the utterances of great leaders. As a result the rank and file, especially in church congregations, are likely to remain out of step for a long time to come. Human indolence is mostly to blame, I suppose. The fact, nevertheless, is that our generation is likely to remain familiar with long disquisitions like the following: "How are we to relate the universal will-form, which as the creation of God is wholly good, to the evil will-form which is called Satan? We are going to say quite frankly and fearlessly that, on the metaphysical plane, this relation presents us with an absolutely irreconcilable dualism." So says Professor Daniel Lamont in his book *Christ and the World of Thought,* highly commended for this declaration by a respected, committed Christian scholar.[3] What is of special concern, moreover, is the general tenor of Lamont's proposed course of action: "It is part of the Christian Revelation to make this theoretical dualism stand out in all its naked obstinacy. Every system which denies the dualism or makes the attempt to cover it up or soften it down is bound to deem evil as in some sense good." Quite a tragic version of "the Christian Revelation"!

It is because of the widespread character of this and similar notions in Christian circles today that the basic attitudes which have come to light throughout these two chapters should be early detected and duly emphasized—those pertaining to the tragic view and to the prophetic view respectively.

This delineation truly cuts across the old "Hebrew-Christian-versus-Greek" divide. It is likely to prove valuable toward further constructive, critical study, which, according to James B. Conant, constitutes the most genuine criterion of scientific research. And yet there is a still brighter prospect at hand—namely, that the new delineation just reached may well spell the ultimate difference between doom and destiny.

15

Doom or Destiny

THE OLD way of interpreting the landscape of reality in terms of the either-Greek-or-Hebrew criterion has proved as irrelevant as it had already proved misleading. The most obvious result of that obsolete criterion has been to set Christianity and modernity into such contrast that they have actually become mighty opposites. So mighty, in fact, that they have been considered mutually exclusive.

If to be a good Christian means to think Hebraically and accordingly to shun the Greek values revived by the Renaissance and nurtured by the Age of Enlightenment, men of culture will have none of it. If, on the other hand, modernity implies turning one's back on a genuinely biblical heritage, then evangelical Christianity will have none of that. Evangelical men will rather utter anew the protest of Tertullian, "What indeed has Athens to do with Jerusalem? . . . We want no curious disputation after possessing Jesus."[1] In the manner of Lactantius and Jerome, they are likely to forego their first love, the love of letters. Thus Lactantius banished Homer as one writing of human rather than divine things, and therefore unable to give information relating to the truth.[2] Jerome, on his part, managed to rule out the three outstanding representatives of Latin literature at one blow: "How can Horace go with the psalter, Virgil with the gospels, Cicero with the apostle?"[3]

Astronomy and cosmology were dismissed by Ambrose of Milan as presumptuous manifestations of heathenism.[4] The renunciation of culture from a genuine and ardently biblical standpoint appears in Bernard of Clairvaux, in Peter Damiani, among the early Franciscans, in Luther, and to a degree even in men like Pascal and Kierkegaard. This dramatic cleavage in fact comes to a climax during the Kierkegaardian period of Karl Barth to the detriment of both modernity and Christianity, henceforth facing each other like Scylla and Charybdis.

After the new delineation suggested by the preceding chapter has been mapped out, however, we are confronted by a propensity on the part of all concerned to be more generally dominated by the tragic viewpoint or by the prophetic, as the case may be. The issue is no longer that of mutually exclusive outlooks in terms of "Greek" modernity versus "Hebrew" Christianity. The actual delineation which now has come to light cuts across both these concerns.

The first net result of this new perspective is that a Christian may in good faith be deeply engaged in all the cultural activities previously associated with modernity. Conversely, a "modern" may freely allow the prophetic outlook to dominate his thought and conversation. Henceforth the age-old conflict between science and religion must be pronounced obsolete. Although the direct aim of the present book has not been to deal with this aspect *per se,* the adventitious conclusion just reached in the course of our exploration is nevertheless precious.

What concerns us directly, however, is the coming to a head of the issue of purpose. The tragic view involves a belief in a necessary, actually fatal course of events, these events being apprehended as moving of their own accord. Granting that the modern scientist has done away with the mythological superstitions once inherent in the conceptions of his ancestors and that he has learned to foresee in order to provide, his plight is nonetheless a pitiable one. The nature which confronts him ultimately seems impervious to his human nature, however corrected and improved it may be by means of new gadgets and mechanical computers.

Much water has gone under the proverbial bridge since the over-optimistic Descartes saw no limits to the mind's apprehension of the physical universe and to the relevance of man's knowledge of it in terms of extension. The physicist nowadays has become aware of a world underlying, but not identical with, that which he observes, as Dirac has shown in *The Principles of Quantum Mechanics*. Of this substratum he cannot form a mental picture without introducing irrelevancies, for the substratum itself is controlled by fundamental laws which do not actually control the world as it appears in our mental picture. Our mental picture is not the true picture. Neither can it ever be, for the true picture is not picturable. This, incidentally, is the reason why the best that can be achieved by the most careful reformulations taking into account the data revealed by an ever improved technology, is the elaboration of such concepts as that of Vaihinger's "useful fiction," to which we have already devoted much attention in these pages.

Fundamental equations, admittedly, need not be picturable. What matters in their case is to know whether picturable conclusions can be derived from them, conclusions which can in turn be tested by means of gross mechanical experiments. This was brought out in a beautiful way when Heinrich Herz "invented" the method coping with the problem posed by Maxwell's theory and identified it with Maxwell's equations. Hence we are led to Duhem's well-taken conclusion that the *experimentum crucis* is impossible in physics. It is the theory as a whole which is verified by the whole body of experimental facts. In these circumstances the experimental verifications do not constitute the foundation of the theory. Rather, they mark its culmination. It may therefore be fairly stated that the contemporary physicist on his own is utterly unable to reach any valid ultimate. In this regard the Kantian critique has been vindicated from the anthropological viewpoint. By the same token it has remained the perfect mental setup for the emergence of a new Promethean race of mortal men. I refer to the double perspective of a realm of noumena sundered from the realm of phenomena.[5]

Indeed modern man lives, moves, and has his being in the long shadow of Kant. The release of extreme forms of idealism, coming to a climax in Hegel and Fichte, those two Promethean heroes of academic philosophy, is contemporary with the immediate impact of Kant. We have already paid tribute to the unique value and relevance of dialectics, particularly as it is germane to a human situation calling for the response of constant statement and restatement in the face of challenging events. Further we may remember William Temple's assurance that what is needed in our time is "a Dialectic more comprehensive and more thorough in its appreciation of the interplay of factors in the real world." This assertion, let us not forget, was made under the necessity of counteracting the dialectical materialism of Marx, Engels, and Lenin. The plain fact, however, is that the dialectical pattern for Marxism has been provided by Hegel and Fichte, and in all these cases the dialectic in question has amounted, not to a candid form of reasoning determined by genuine encounters with facts, but actually to a *dramatization* of the dialectical process. We may identify a Promethean process in each instance of this dramatization.

Hegel's new academic trinity of Thesis, Antithesis, and Synthesis was more than a gratuitous postulation of the process according to which the Idea or Spirit comes into its own. It actually stood for a Promethean heaven storming. And it was so understood by the most distinguished disciple Hegel ever had in France, namely, Ernest Renan. Declared Renan, "God does not exist as yet, but he might exist some day"—that is, I suppose, once a Hegelian Prometheus has reached the very top of the idealistic scaffolding with his own torch flaming. This, in effect, was an improvement on the myth and even on its first great dramatizer, Aeschylus.

The Promethean character of Fichte is, if possible, more ominous still. Fichte's absolute ego required an obstacle to overcome in order to sharpen its powers. Subsequently all checks upon truth had to be removed as well as all checks upon genuine reverence, that greatest of all qualities essential to the life of the mind. This was the fullness of Promethean defiance. What came forth in and through such pseudo-divine madness was an intoxication of power amounting to cosmic impiety.[6]

What, then, shall I say of the Marxist counterpart if not that with Lenin, Stalin, and their stooges, it turned into a sneering parody of religion which could be only mildly suggested by the concluding movement of the *Fantastic Symphony* of Berlioz. As the strains of a distorted *Dies Irae* and the pealing of broken bells mount up defiantly amid the shrieks of witches, the proper mood is set for assessing the sinister picture that Russian Communism, with its parody of religion, offers to our generation. I mean its arrogant manifestos as scriptures, its messiah in Stalinian garb, its worship of an embalmed Lenin, the rule of its party bosses featured by Khrushchev, with Malenkov cast in the role of Judas and overt Communists, "fifth columnists," and other fellow travelers as apostles and missionaries. Indeed it remained for our age to provide this distorted collective version of Promethean defiance!

But to pass on to less repulsive illustrations of Promethean infiltration of both modernity and Christianity. The rise of Romanticism also, in the most varied realms of life and thought, is contemporary with the immediate impact of Kant. Admittedly, the movement as a whole has more complex origins and manifestations. The fact that Romanticism steps forward to the front of the stage beneath the sign of the French Revolution only adds to its Promethean character. A many-sided European political Romanticism belongs in the picture I am sketching. To give but one illustration, is not Napoleon a most impressive incarnation of a modern, heaven-storming hero wont to hide his immense ambition under highly ideological motives? His calculated exploitation of the liberal Auteuil Society together with its counterpart the Society of Philadelphia (now the American Philosophical Society) leaves no doubt on the subject. Should any such doubt be left, moreover, the reading of the St. Helena Memorial, where the exiled Napoleon actually rewrote history in terms of Ideology, would soon dispel it.

As the romantic characters step forward on the stage "clad in Hell-fire," to use Carlyle's powerful phrase, a Satanic strain appears unmistakably in their countenance. Just as Milton's Satan has been identified as a personification of the English Revolution, one senses in the Satanic nature of the romantic hero at least a reflection of the great French upheaval. There is in him a strange obdurateness mingled with enthusiasm, a rebellious pride parading as committed liberal independence. The main reason the Middle Ages particularly tempted the romantics, Goethe, Chateaubriand, and Walter Scott helping, is that the medieval period had been the Golden Age of the devil. In this respect, Victor Hugo could rightly identify chivalry with deviltry.

The Britannic and Puritan Satan was in essence the anti-God whom Milton plunged into eternal confinement. This suggestion of a revolted spirit notably increased Satan's Promethean value. The Germans, under the spell of Goethe's Faust, had stressed the human side of the devil, thus doing an injustice to his angelic nature. From the rather heavy Germanic Mephistopheles, the French first tended to create a national Méphisto who was light, fashionable, artistic, and slightly bohemian, resembling Don Juan,

Gavroche, d'Artagnan, and Cyrano. Soon, however, the personification took on deeper Promethean overtones.

The romantics were proud rebels who considered themselves misunderstood geniuses. There lurked an affectation of nihilism among these malcontents. They refused to yield to law, discontent with the age because discontent with themselves. In Satan they found some of their own fatalism, their own defiant frustration. From thence arose the poetic meaning of the bandit, the outlaw, personified with such success in the characters of Ruy Blas and Hernani. Like themselves, their Satan deserved sympathy. He was a cursed hero in revolt, who suffered for a worthy cause and accordingly was worthy of an admiring sympathy. His damnation seemed excessive. And so the romantics revised his sentence under various titles and in their own way rewrote *Paradise Lost*. These titles in fact are legion in terms of comparative literature all over Europe. Painted in flattering colors, Satan also became irresistible because of his cryptic nature adorned in beautiful Byronic somberness. And what a Promethean hero Byron himself turned out to be! The mystery of his soul had the delicious lure of an abyss whose depths the daring felt tempted to sound. The same strain is present in Blake's vision of a blasphemous Antichrist, hater of dignities, lover of wild rebellion, and transgressor of God's law. Also in Nietzsche's assumed will-to-power and self-aggrandizement as the all-embracing principle and motivation of the rise of man. Again, in our day, in Sartre's exaltation of "the defiant man" of Kierkegaard.

In the long run, Satan became to the romantics an immense symbol of cosmic evil, a sort of Angra Mainyu whose activities were at one with those of the forces of nature. He was to be found in the fatality of things moving of their own accord, in the brutal dynamism of matter, in the sobbing wind as in the raging tempest, in falling night as in coming death. Satan was the rebellious bitterness at the bottom of our joys; he was the hybrid sensation that emerges out of unresigned nothingness. Satan was again in the frustrating promises that lie, in the deceiving happiness that ends in doom. He was *the* romantic hero, calling for recognition under a leaded sky; a defeated Prometheus who had challenged heaven only to encounter an impassible heaven that was dumb in its steellike coldness. Surely there was no kind of purpose to be disclosed to mortal man from "up there"! Henceforth the only possible diversion in the Pascalian sense of the word seemed to be found solely in an inverse grace amounting to the certainty of wrongdoing. This is forcefully suggested in the private diaries and letters of the most genial, most deeply wounded of all romantic heroes—the one who opened his *Flowers of Evil* with this dedication to the reader:

—To thee, hypocrite,—my fellow-creature,—my brother!

I mean Baudelaire.

The forms of cosmic impiety just detected in the realms of philosophy, politics, and literature, as they unfold in the long shadow of Kant, have also become apparent in the field of theological thought, as the next chapter will show. We have here a vindication of the conclusions forced upon us: that the delineation between essentially tragic elements and essentially prophetic elements cuts clear across the old Greek-versus-Hebrew cleavage; and that the tragic view is the mainspring of the sense of purposelessness so prevalent in our modern age. And since the presence of this mainspring is also detected in the realm of theological thinking, it is clear that a genuine recovery of purpose implies a reconceived Christianity.

16

Ego or Purpose

It now appears that the Barthian critique of Schleiermacher, however penetrating its insights may have proved, has not reached the core of the issue at hand. Schleiermacher, let it be remembered, had singled out as the essence of religion, the unique, pious feeling of absolute dependence awakened in his consciousness by the experience of universal existence. His own soul was in the bosom of nature. As we dwell on the immediate implications of his sense of participation, we detect in it at least two converse elements—namely, the religious feeling of piety and an egocentric sense of personal uniqueness. As these were germane to each other, they easily fused into one in the beautiful soul of Schleiermacher. The point is, however, that they proceeded mostly from two different sources.

Clearly, the element of piety was an original feature. It had been inherited from the devotional spirituality which the former pupil had so deeply assimilated at the Niesky Moravian school. Did he not admit as much when he said in later years that to him a basic Moravian view was close to being the ideal in Christian life and conversation? Granting that a certain degree of personalism is inherent in this theology of feeling, the very sense of dependence involved in the experience is likely to bring it under strict control, if not to eliminate its egocentric character. Therefore, the unmistakable strain of egocentricity detected at the very core of Schleiermacher's experience actually seems to proceed from another source.

We need not seek far for it. When the young man moved from Halle where he had plunged into an intensive study of Kant, he went to Berlin where he became a fervent, enthusiastic adept of Romanticism. Henceforth his religious views became in a real way the theological expression of Romanticism, or, if you prefer, a romantic expression of theology. The somewhat defiant *Discourses on Religion to Its Cultured Despisers,* and still more the *Soliloquies* published soon after, bear testimony to this fresh apprehension of the pietistic experience.

Henceforth, the competence of the ego is emphasized in a romantic view. The defiance of biblical doctrines becomes an overtone, and they are freely exposed as not essentially religious of themselves. This accounts, at least in part, for the fact that even in Schleiermacher's great dogmatic work *The Christian Faith,* the sense of a historical revelation of God in Christ remains weak, as does his sense of the controlling power of Christian life throughout the ages. The Old Testament fares worse still. He never acknowledges it as conveying a divine dispensation. Broadly speaking, the introspection of Schleiermacher never amounts to an encounter with the living God of Scripture mediated by Church and Sacrament. Rather he suggests his experience in terms of the Platonic relationship which this visible world holds to the Ideas. It is essentially in Plato, in fact, that the human spirit received the classical expression of its self-transcendence. There is further present in Schleiermacher the Platonic sense that the notions this transcendence conveys call for a degree of factual verification. This accounts for the undeniable scientific strain which runs across the whole theology of a man who had fervently translated Plato and lectured on Greek philosophy.

I have always felt that the reason people generally fail to see through the deceptive character of man-made views is that these views have the knack of living "on the principal." Thus the utopia of collectivism is likely to thrive for an appreciable length of time on the wealth accumulated through generations—hence the illusion that collectivism is actually producing a decent, if not high, standard of living. So too with utopia in religion. It seems to remain close to the truth which is God because it still stands close in time to a godly heritage. This would seem to have been the case for the theology of feeling inseparable from the name of Schleiermacher. Once treasures of genuine piety had dissipated and new generations intervened, the pietistic element in the religious life of Schleiermacher faded away. There remained essentially the egocentric, romantic element with all its sharp angles. Once more Prometheus stepped forward to the front of the stage, this time in theological garb.

The Promethean element inherent in a religious individualism cut loose from the control of the Apostolic faith was bound to emerge sooner or later. And so it did as soon as newly released forms of religious romanticism became dramatized in terms of Hegelian idealism. I refer especially to the days when Hegel ridiculed the identification of true religion with the feeling of absolute dependence. If it be so, he said, then the dog may be acknowledged as the model a religious man should emulate. I have always felt that in making this assertion Hegel was quite unfair to the dog. By then Hegel was well on his way to devising the Promethean concepts the baleful impact of which already has been pointed out.

The merging of the theology of feeling with philosophical idealism has been further aggravated by the coming together of the notion of progress originally worked out by political scientists, and the notion of Darwinian evolution originally wrought out in a biological setting. It is fascinating in a way to follow in detail the manner in which these two notions have emerged from entirely different realms to be absorbed into the new faith-principle of Evolution-Progress, truly the Promethean principle of the Rise of Man. And further, to ascertain the ways in which this same faith-principle has been called upon to provide a most unexpected framework for recasting biblical material. Thus David Strauss, a disciple of both Hegel and Baur, attempted in his later writings to straighten out some of the constructions put upon the life of Jesus by Schleiermacher. He meant to improve them by harmonizing idealism with Darwinism within the framework of a positive materialism—the religious counterpart of the Marxian reinterpretation of Hegel. Feuerbach, a "left-winger" of the Hegelian school, similarly took Hegel to task for having done great injustice to the element of sensation. He also ended by propounding materialistic views, to a point where religion was reduced to the mere projection of man's own nature and ideals.[1] A contemporary terminus of this procedure appears in myth-generating father symbols, mother symbols, and combined father-mother symbols, which make over the world in which we live in the image of their human originators. Yet to Feuerbach already, man was the beginning, the center, and the end of religion. A defiant negativism could hardly have gone further, under God's high heaven. Anthropocentric religion truly has come into its own with Feuerbach.

New forms of "high religion" have appeared in the wake of this naturism. They may be freely detected in the perverted transcendentalism of James Joyce, as well as in the mystic cosmology of D. H. Lawrence. Possibly they find their most characteristic expression in our day in the dynamism of "the Eternal Gospel" according to Gerald Heard. This, I want to make clear, is said with due regard for the real contribution this pioneer has otherwise made to contemporary religious thought. But the story is somewhat different when the author of *The Eternal Gospel* suggests a procedure amounting to a Promethean quest. He would in effect have us enter the den of Doctor Faustus or join the impassioned Claude Frollo as the latter blows his bellows in one of the towers of Notre Dame, except that we live in the second part of the twentieth century. Yet the language is the same, and it is a Promethean form of language, "To get to the nucleus of the atom, to hit and break it there is needed an immense electric charge. . . ." It naturally follows that, "If the soul is to be transmuted, a charge of spiritual force as high, and as dangerous if lightly handled, is required. We are not getting these results in the spiritual realm. Why?" Thus spoke the alchemist of old who, having exhausted the *fas* of knowledge, finally dared to penetrate the *nefas* to steal again the heavenly fire in a heaven-storming thrust. Impatience is dangerous in such matters, for one whose admitted ideal is to become "a thing with a head."[2] No wonder *The Saturday Review* characterized the author's following work, a novel, as "this strange and terrible book . . . as repellently fascinating as the discovery of a cobra in one's bed."[3]

To pass such judgments seemingly amounts to a reversion to the days when the man of science came under suspicion for the sole reason that he was a man of science. And yet there is more at stake here than meets the eye. Once an objective approach has reduced access to truth to a scientific quest, and even purged it from its most obvious romantic and otherwise Promethean overtones, the end product nevertheless remains Promethean in essence and therefore pertains to the tragic view—the purposeless view.

There is deep truth in the assertion Alfred North Whitehead has made in the opening chapter of *Science and the Modern World*. The vision of the great tragedians of ancient Athens, Aeschylus, Sophocles, and Euripides, "is the vision possessed by science. Fate

in Greek Tragedy becomes the order of nature in modern thought."
According to this vision, fate is remorseless and indifferent. It
urges "a tragic incident to its inevitable issue." Therein lies the
"remorseless inevitableness" which pervades scientific thought.
"The laws of physics are the decrees of fate."[4]

Only an awareness of this situation may have led us to detect
and appreciate the constructive character of the insights of Karl
Barth. Yet the task now remains to expose the tragic character of
the dichotomy his extreme reaction against Schleiermacher has led
him to assume. As far as I have been able to find out, Barth himself has remained unaware of this specific aspect in his contribution. Indeed his critique of Schleiermacher indirectly has come to
grips with whatever Promethean elements our preceding pages
have detected in it. The trouble, however, is that in the fire of
controversy Karl Barth has, at least during his Kierkegaardian
period, reinstated a "mighty opposites" type of situation stressing
the wholly-Otherness of the living God. Even the radicalism with
which he continues to insist that there is no way whatsoever from
anthropology to theology shows that he has not fully realized the
true Promethean nature of the danger at hand. For there does appear a way from anthropology to theology the moment the alternative at hand is seen to be, not between Hebrew and Greek, but
rather between the prophetic view and the tragic view.

The prophetic view actually provides a firm, dynamic orientation for a man of goodwill proceeding from anthropology to
theology. And this man's progress is bound to become ever firmer
as he comes to realize that, far from assuming the age-old
"Hebrew-versus-Greek" cleavage, the prophetic view implies its
deletion. The realm of creation is not incompatible with the nature
of its Creator. Whatever discrepancy or alienation may appear between Creator and creature, moreover, is not specifically scientific
or metaphysical in character. It amounts to disparity in terms of

righteousness and unrighteousness. And this disparity appears more as a matter of degree than of contrast. All the more so because God knows man to be subject to temptation. It is not for mortal man to pass judgment on such matters; he is only too prone to error. " 'Judgment is mine,' saith the Lord." Would to God all Christians could see things accordingly, for that is just the meaning of our Lord's scathing condemnation of Pharisaism.

The danger inherent in failing to grant these implications of the prophetic view while insisting on a Calvinistic dichotomy is that of promoting a resurgence of virulent Christian versions of the very sin of *hubris*. Thus Brunner's dramatic presentation of *Man in Revolt*, in spite of its undeniably high qualities, also has clear Promethean overtones. Such a presentation is pessimistic in essence, just as the tragic view is, and for basically the same reason. The charter of a genuine Christian enlightenment has found a most adequate expression in Professor Hendry's reminder that "the Holy Spirit does not annihilate our spirits, but bears witness with our spirits."[5]

A further corrective of the Barthian critique of Schleiermacher now suggests itself. I have insisted on a basic similitude between the tragic view and the anthropocentric view. It now appears that this similitude does not amount to final identity. The primary element here is not merely the human element as such. It is the human element as it has been contaminated by the tragic view. Religiously speaking, the kind of anthropomorphism we need to expose is *Promethean* anthropomorphism.

In the final analysis it is the Prometheus who slumbers in the soul of "every man that cometh into the world," who is responsible for the loss of man's true Purpose. The reason is that Prometheus stands for man definitely and stubbornly on his own. Not necessarily a man without purpose, mind you. A man has always some kind of purpose for doing what he does. Yet in the case of a Prometheus, this purpose, whatever it may be, is likely to be fiercely and mercilessly contended for out of motives which may at times betray high nobility. Were it not so, he would not be Prometheus.

The fact remains, nevertheless, that because Prometheus *per se* is a man utterly on his own, the God of Jesus Christ is to this man as if he were not. And this, according to the prophetic view, is the essence of all sin because it involves disloyalty to the All-Loving, who "gave his only begotten Son, that whosoever believeth in him should not perish, but have everlasting life." Seen in the Light shining on the Cross, sin is what it is in all its ugliness because of what God has done in Christ. The significance of his Act meets everyone within a single human perspective in a language common to all. And this is what makes the prophetic view so profoundly different from the tragic view and its double perspective.

Here at last we may understand why the basic difficulty involved in accepting the Gospel is not specifically a matter of content; it is not to be stated in terms of "what a man can believe." Neither may it be solved in terms of "demythologizing." Any kind of "demythologizing" likely to prove pertinent should come by way of implication. Obsolete notions, like old soldiers, never die; they just fade away. And so "demythologizing" can never be an end in itself. The reason the Gospel is difficult to accept is that the acceptance involves the surrender of the Promethean in man; that is, the surrender of all that makes him believe in his own intrinsic nobility, in the intrinsic rightness of his self-appointed tasks; in his unquestioned ability "to make it on his own," and unreservedly get full credit for the stunt.

This, in essence, is the tragic view, the view that spells utter denial of the true Purpose of life. It is the view from which we may be delivered only by the Gospel. And the Gospel is what it is in its uniqueness because it provides the only possible deliverance from that baleful view. To see the matter in this light and then to proceed on what has been seen, is to have shifted from doom to destiny; to be on one's way to *becoming* a Christian, as Kierkegaard would say.

Conclusion

A SENSE of cosmic purpose painstakingly secured over thousands of years, thanks mostly to the Gospel, has again been lost. Our Western world accordingly has reverted to a mood of futility and even to the very forms of doom which so tragically characterized its ancient days. In these circumstances, it has appeared that only a reconception of the religion which had originally set forth and provided the true Purpose could once more restore it to a needy world![1] Seen in this light the recovery of purpose and the reconception of Christianity respectively are but two aspects of one and the same want. It was to be expected that as our inquiry progressed, the solidarity between loss of purpose on the part of modernity, and failure on the part of Christianity to cope with the resulting plight, should prove ever more marked. And so, proceeding upon this clue, we have found that far from standing at opposite poles, both modernity and Christianity actually labor under one and the same delusion. The common woe which has afflicted them all along has been traced back to anthropocentric ways of apprehending reality. These ways in turn have proved inseparable from Promethean leanings inherent in the tragic view and coming to expression in the classical sin of *hubris*.

The only possible restoration in the face of this situation has appeared in a conversion from the tragic, Promethean outlook to the prophetic outlook. This outlook is dominated by the consideration that in the last analysis our plight does not pertain to a situation of double perspective and mighty opposites. It must be ascribed to a basic confusion inherent in man's alienation from his heavenly Father, and conversely from his true self. Hence the loss of the one and only Purpose identified with the Living God, who is the Principle and End of all things.

Probably the deepest insight into the prophetic attitude is mediated in the biblical insistence on God's nearness to man, a theme which runs from prophet and Psalmist to our Lord himself, and from him to the culmination of Paul's eighth chapter of *Romans*. I think first of Psalm 139:

> O Lord, thou hast searched me, and known me.
> Thou knowest my downsitting and mine uprising,
>> thou understandest my thought afar off.
> Thou compassest my path and my lying down,
>> and art acquainted with all my ways.
> For there is not a word in my tongue,
>> but, lo, O Lord, thou knowest it altogether.
> Thou hast beset me behind and before,
>> and laid thine hand upon me. . . .
> Whither shall I go from thy spirit?
>> or whither shall I flee from thy presence?
> If I ascend up into heaven, thou art there:
>> if I make my bed in hell, behold, thou art there.
> If I take the wings of the morning,
>> and dwell in the uttermost parts of the sea;
> Even there shall thy hand lead me,
>> and thy right hand shall hold me.
> If I say, Surely the darkness shall cover me;
>> even the night shall be light about me.
> Yea, the darkness hideth not from thee;
>> but the night shineth as the day:
>> the darkness and the light are both alike to thee.

This is truly the charter of Purpose. Its implications find expression in the Sermon on the Mount, more especially in these words of our Lord, recorded in Matt. 6:25–34:

Therefore I say unto you, Take no thought for your life, what ye shall eat, or what ye shall drink; nor yet for your body, what ye shall put on. Is not the life more than meat, and the body than raiment?

Behold the fowls of the air: for they sow not, neither do they reap, nor gather into barns; yet your heavenly Father feedeth them. Are ye not much better than they? . . .

And why take ye thought for raiment? Consider the lilies of the field, how they grow; they toil not, neither do they spin:

And yet I say unto you, That even Solomon in all his glory was not arrayed like one of these.

Wherefore, if God so clothe the grass of the field, which today is, and tomorrow is cast into the oven, shall he not much more clothe you, O ye of little faith?

Therefore take no thought, saying, What shall we eat? or, What shall we drink? or, Wherewithal shall we be clothed?

. . . for your heavenly Father knoweth that ye have need of all these things.

But seek ye first the kingdom of God, and his righteousness; and all these things shall be added unto you.

Take therefore no thought for the morrow: for the morrow shall take thought for the things of itself. Sufficient unto the day is the evil thereof.

We have by now reached the mountaintop of the biblical disclosure of Purpose and of the meaningfulness of a godly life. Hence the summation of the meaning of life, once Purpose has been recovered, in I Pet. 5:7, "Casting all your care upon him; for he careth for you." And the glorious hallelujah of Paul in the concluding "movement" of Romans 8:

Who shall separate us from the love of Christ? Shall tribulation, or distress, or persecution, or famine, or nakedness, or peril, or sword? . . .

Nay, in all these things we are more than conquerors through him that loved us.

For I am persuaded, that neither death, nor life, nor angels, nor principalities, nor powers, nor things present, nor things to come,

Nor height, nor depth, nor any other creature, shall be able to separate us from the love of God, which is in Christ Jesus our Lord.

These capital texts blaze the trail of light that so safely and triumphantly points the way of Purpose across our wilderness— the way of the prophetic trail.

Modernity has been missing the mark, then, not so much because of a liberalism swayed by secular world views. But rather because of modernity's surrender to the tragic view, as the classical sin of *hubris* was allowed to contaminate the scriptural notion of sin, that of a prodigal son's alienation from an all-loving God.

In acknowledging this, however, we must admit that current views of Christianity stand condemned on a par with corresponding views in modernity. Granting that the story of the Fall in the Book of Genesis does suggest a biblical version of *hubris* as self-sufficiency or pride, the current insistence upon its dramatic, fatal character pertains more to the tragic view than to the prophetic. So does *a fortiori* the concept of original sin in terms of original guilt. And so, to a higher degree, does Augustine's corporate notion of mankind as a "sinful mass" (*massa peccatrix*) laboring under an eternal curse. The reason sin has thus taken tragic overtones in evangelical circles today is that the dramatic building up of Satan as the Ruler of a world of Darkness, standing on a par with God as the mighty opposite of God and his world of Light, has affected the more sober biblical view. Milton unconsciously may have had a share in emphasizing the inherent dualism of Lucifer and Prometheus. According to R. J. Z. Werblowsky, this dualism would seem to suggest both the Hebraic and Greek versions of the birth of human consciousness. Perhaps his theory accounts for the hybridic character of a civilization at times characterized as an invention of the devil.[2]

What we have in the opening pages of the Book of Genesis is a vivid presentation of man's eternal plight—namely, that one created to live in fellowship with God chooses to keep away from God, and this in a created world where the God of the 139th Psalm is nearer to his children than hands and feet. No cleavage, no irresolvable antinomy is at stake in this situation, no fatal necessity. The heavenly Father of his prodigal sons has overruled it in Jesus Christ. To see things otherwise is to read the tragic view back into Scripture, with the result that unbearable guilt complexes become conducive to unhealthy introspection and even to subsequent personality breakdowns. Another deplorable outcome is likely to be a false humility which takes pride in not being proud. The fact is that our Christian circles today are plagued by attitudes of constrained self-debasement, which border more on the pathological than on the evangelical. True Christian humility is the humility of a son, humility before God.

Even the notion of salvation has been spoiled by the ever-recurring infiltration of tragic views. Thus alienation from God is easily transposed into terms of a man being doomed like an animal caught in a trap. Such a tragic situation is well illustrated in the drama of Ibsen, for example. Thus in *A Doll's House,* the recurrent theme is that of unavoidable self-assertion, followed by release at any cost once fatal consequences have caught up with the helpless victim. Phrases abound to that effect, such as: "I want to get on . . ."; "I had to do it . . ."; "You came and stood in my way." Mrs. Linde "had to break" with Krogstad. Krogstad had to clear his reputation. He had "means to compel" Nora. Nora, in her turn, had been forced to do what she had done to save the life of her husband. Now that she was "caught," she stood horror-stricken, "as if rooted to the spot," and whispered, "No, not that!

Never, never! Anything rather than that! Oh! for some way out of it!"[3]

Are these the trappings to be used to convince the recalcitrant that he had better "make a decision for Christ" right here and now—or else? Alas, the theme of Jonathan Edwards' sermon "Sinners in the Hands of an Angry God" is still very much alive in popular evangelism today. I quote from the peroration:

And you, children, who are unconverted, do not you know that you are going down to hell, to bear the dreadful wrath of that God, who is now angry with you every day and every night? . . .

And let every one that is out of Christ, and hanging over the pit of hell, whether they be old men and women, or middle aged, or young people, or little children, now hearken to the loud calls of God's word and providence. . . .

Therefore, let every one that is out of Christ, now awake and fly from the wrath to come. The wrath of Almighty God is now undoubtedly hanging over a great part of this congregation. . . .[4]

An overemphasis on the Ransom theory of atonement suggested by Origen, then further emphasized in the Middle Ages by Anselm in terms of satisfaction that should be rendered to one's overlord, similarly propounds the tragic view. No wonder Albert Schweitzer exposed it as "this completely unsatisfactory explanation."[5] There is no doubt that it has alienated multitudes from the Gospel. Were we to remember that the word "gospel" means "good news," we would accordingly take sides with William Tyndale, who, in his *Prologue to the New Testament* (1525), characterized Christianity as

good, mery
glad and joyfull tydings, that maketh a
mannes hert glad, and maketh hym synge,
daunce and leepe for ioye.

For this view of Tyndale is the prophetic view, the genuinely Christian view.

What we need, then—if I may beg leave to coin another of the awful neologisms current in our day—is not so much "demythologizing" as it is "detragicizing." My justification is that while "demythologizing" the Gospel is likely to transmute it into a mass of dried bones, "detragicizing" current forms of evangelism is sure to restore the Gospel to the pristine glory hailed by William Tyndale. I need not insist that these conclusions apply to the Christian landscape of reality as a whole, that is, to the world of nature and of man as beheld with Christian eyes.

The tragic outlook is a radically pessimistic, a calamitous outlook —the outlook of a long-faced Christianity. I, for one, shudder each time a preacher takes on that look to intone lugubriously the invitation, "Let us pray," as if praying were the most dreadful thing a man could ever do. The prayer which conveys the tragic outlook is certainly more in the nature of *De Profundis* than of *Laudamus Domine*. There is a certain kind of evangelicalism which seems to exult in the darkest aspects of life. The darker, the better, it would seem. The tragic mood is further expressed in a propensity to account for calamities in terms of "what was to be expected in the situation." Certain concepts of God and creation are conveyed through interpretations of great cataclysms which reduce them to the matter-of-course character of easily accountable happenings. So the book of Revelation has freely been used in recent times to rationalize the most dreadful developments in the realm of nuclear warfare.

I bring to a close these admittedly unpleasant considerations by drawing attention to more trivial manifestations of the same order. I refer especially to instances of a Pharisaism bordering on what the Germans call *Schadenfreude*, that insidious joy certain people seem to feel in detecting damaging features. I cannot help but detect something of this mood in an "edifying" poem entitled, "The Clean Amid the Unclean," which was recently brought to my attention. This bit of poetry proceeds upon the now familiar double perspective within the framework of a dramatized contrast:

Flowers of the purest white,
That sweetest fragrance bear,
Bloom in the midst of darkness and decay;
The water lily, clothed in light,
And fair, doth yet appear
From out the filth and mire, and grace portray.

. . .

So may we also walk
Amid the sin of the earth,
As luminaries, bearing heaven's light,
And hold the torch of Him, our Lord;
For where is righteousness
More needed than in drear and darkest night?

I leave it to the reader to evaluate further this all too familiar type of production which may hardly be said to contribute to the propagation of the Gospel.

Such features in many ways testify to more harmful concessions to the nature of things on the part of Christianity than the loudly exposed "capitulations" to modernism ever did. The *contemptus mundi* to which they bear witness no longer expresses that loosening from earthly attachments and ambitions, initiated deep within by the stirrings of divine love. It is no longer *contemptus mundi* in the hallowed, long-established sense. It has now literally become *contemptus* pure and simple, in the revived tragic context.

Look at it as we may the essential difficulty across the path of the Gospel is the difficulty a man encounters at tearing himself loose from the Prometheus who slumbers at the very core of his being. It is not essentially that of a reluctance to believe this miracle or that Gospel story. Scholars like Hoskyns and Davey suggest that the New Testament account of a given miracle may actually constitute the dramatization of a story. Even so, if any element is to be taken to task in that miracle, it is once more the element of drama. In such a case, however, the dramatization is mild enough, and further it is in the right direction, that of prophetic interpretation. This is strongly suggested for example in the case of the parable of the fig tree told in Luke 13:6-9, when viewed as the possible source of the account of the miraculous cursing of the fig tree (Matt. 21:19-21; Mark 11:12-14, 20, 21). The dominant consideration in both cases is not so much that of the actual historicity of the miracle, as it is the prophetic, Christological interpretation inherent in both.[6] To "demythologize" the account of the miracle not only misses the point, but amounts to eliminating those elements in the miracle which served to emphasize the significance of the teaching originally conveyed in and through the parable. It amounts to "throwing out the baby with the bath." Clearly, what is primary in the New Testament record is a Christology which has inspired and oriented it at every point. Seen in this light the Gospel miracles constitute a unique pattern of revelation and are true in the deepest meaning of the word.

Surely this is the place to remember that truth, in the prophetic meaning of the term, is truth grounded in the reliability of God. This is why it is live truth, truth to be done by those who would know with certainty, truth adequate to Purpose because it is the Purpose-bearing truth.

Modern science has felt constrained to discard the element of purpose for the sake of intellectual honesty. Finality, in particular, has been rejected, for it essentially pertains to empirical, anthropomorphic notions of causality devised by the Phenomenal Man at his own human level. But it has now become clear, I hope, that these elements have nothing in common with the God-given truth just asserted.

In his epoch-making controversy with Lord Samuel, Einstein has taught us that far from continuing to establish analogies between new phenomena and the familiar phenomena of daily experience, the informed scientist has learned to distrust and finally shun such analogies. It has appeared to him that the correspondence or correlation between our concepts and our sensations becomes all the more indirect as purer mental models are devised. As these mental models are perfected and applied to the world of sense experience, they do indeed become all the more remote from the familiar, empirical data of consciousness. Yet it is this very remoteness which allows a closer, more adequate approximation of this world. Hence an imperative caveat with regard to man-made "truth." Once this modern scientific trend reaches its consummation, we will be confronted by a symbolic logic in which both logic and pure mathematics derived from it, are fused into one single grammar of analytical concepts of an ultimately nonreferential character.

In the light of these developments, the tragic views of men like Bertrand Russell and Professor W. T. Stace stand exposed. These men in fact have fallen victims to their own devices—and we say it without casting the slightest shadow upon the excellence of these devices. These devices actually involved a final dismissal of the empirical, anthropomorphic ways of Aristotelian causality, with special reference to finality. What they did not, and could not possibly involve, was any kind of interference with the biblical, prophetic view of Purpose with a capital P.

Once this conclusion has been granted, not only does the pseudo-tension usually postulated between modernity and Christianity fade away, but modernity proves to have rendered inestimable service to theology. Henceforth, the path has been cleared for a common indictment of anthropocentric ways in theology as well as in the other sciences. It has become possible to ascribe full value and relevance to the Barthian rediscovery of Anselm and to his subsequent critique of Schleiermacher, even though exception be taken to Barth's partial reversal to the tragic view.

In this concluding part where I mean to point the way to further research, I find myself in a position to say more. Because the scientific methods at their best are increasingly amounting to neutral, colorless, and accordingly impartial ways of approach, theology may put them to full use. There we may expect them to prove as purifying with regard to essentially anthropocentric notions, as they have proved in other realms. A genuine science of biblical facts accordingly is now coming into its own. It holds the promise of purging Christianity from the accretion of foreign elements while blazing the trail for an adequate reconception. I am not suggesting that methods successfully applied in the realm of the natural sciences can merely be extended to other realms or in any way generalized. Even the ancients were aware of this danger, and I have already made allowance for it.

In the application of the historical method, consider the constructive character of biblical interpretation at its best. Here is a field in which we can learn more from the natural sciences than we have done heretofore, without ever forcing upon the Bible categories foreign to its make-up. Now that a great deal of prejudice against modernity has been cleared up and the possibility and advisability of closer co-operation have been acknowledged, we may safely think of making the most of the constructive method so widely used in scientific work today. The justification for doing so has just been recalled to our attention in the case of Einstein. The late physicist pointed out that in spite of their apparent remoteness, the mental models elaborated by the scientist actually allow a closer, more adequate interpretation of the data at hand. We have no *a priori* reason to believe that a comparable situation may not arise in theology, in this case with reference to God's time since Christianity is essentially a historical religion.

As soon as the matter is considered in this way, we cannot but be impressed by the fact that past events recorded by the sacred writers become meaningful essentially with regard to their present significance for us today. In this connection they do not so much stay "back there," as cast their meaning into the future. This unusual situation has been oddly, yet accurately suggested in a phrase coined by Nels Ferré, "the is-ness of the was."

Here then is a clue to constructive thinking in biblical interpretation: the model we need has been provided. And the biblical revelation is what it is because it has disclosed what otherwise should have become the object of a mental construction on the part of the theologian.

The model is a prophetic one. It makes for the unique perspective without which the history of Israel would read like the histories of other peoples, except that it would in most cases be far less significant than theirs. The perspective is that which the prophets of Israel had on the course of events, and according to which these events were presented. In other words this same perspective is determined by a unique vantage point set apart from the many vantage points secular historians might elect—one writing history from an economic standpoint for example, others from some theoretical viewpoint of their own.

The uniqueness of the model may accordingly be said to lie in the fact that it conditions the true vision—namely, the vision of faith. Faith is just as essential to right perception as the faculty of sight is to the functioning of the eye. Paul S. Minear has happily entitled one of his best books, a study in the biblical point of view, *Eyes of Faith*. In a striking Introduction he has stated that the following five points have increasingly impressed him:

(1) the strangeness of the Biblical perspective; (2) the unity of this perspective throughout the Biblical period; (3) the futility of trying to understand any segment of thought detached from its hidden context; (4) the germinal power and universal relevance that emerges whenever that context is uncovered and appropriated; (5) the unsuspected value of the most objectionable patterns of thought in locating distinctive dimensions.

What has impressed me still more if possible than these five points, is the personal confession which followed upon them:

I may say that each of these convictions has been forced upon me against my own inclination; when I started the study of the New Testament I had almost the opposite expectations. Over and over again, I have been chagrined to have my convictions reversed. When I have been most certain that I understood Isaiah or Jesus, because a particular teaching seemed to agree with my fund of opinions, I have in fact been farthest from understanding them. . . . And finally the suspicion dawned that perhaps the strange history within which the apostle stood *is* the true history within which I too stand.[7]

An elaboration on the two preceding quotations might be close to a running commentary on some of the conclusions now in the process of recapitulation. With special reference to the matter immediately at hand, the vision made possible by "eyes of faith" has been clearly singled out and contrasted to currently accepted man-made views—to those which in a particular teaching "seemed to agree with my fund of opinions."

In his *God Was in Christ,* already a classic, D. M. Baillie has confessed to a degree of uneasiness at the curious combination of theological dogmatism and historical skepticism so noticeable in men like Rudolf Bultmann. Do not such endeavors in theology amount to so many attempts to "gather apologetic figs from skeptical thistles," as Harnack once put the matter to the young Friedrich Loofs? Baillie suggests the beginning of a solution as follows:

It seems to me that a good deal of confusion would be averted if we reminded ourselves that the phrase "the Jesus of history" means simply and precisely: "Jesus as He really was in His life on earth," which includes of course what He did and said, what He intended and what He thought. The phrase does usually imply that in certain respects we must give a different account of this from what was given in the pre-critical period, but that will be pretty generally recognized.[8]

The present inquiry suggests that more yet is at stake in this matter than the closer apprehension of past events made possible by modern historical methods. The same conclusion is forced upon us when, a few pages further, Baillie takes Barth's theology to task for having so austerely become a theology of the Word that "it is hardly a theology of the Word-made-flesh."[9] Baillie is alluding to a type of confusion repeatedly pointed out in these pages, a confusion between biblical experience and theological understanding —between the empirical data of actual life at the human level on the one hand, and on the other the mental constructs meant to conceive that same life more adequately. A failure to heed the resulting tension may result in theological interpretation conditioned by personal feeling, that is, in types of theology reminiscent of the heydays of empiricism. I know of no better illustration of this than Martin Luther.

As the great Lutheran scholar Henri Strohl of the University of Strasbourg has restated the case,[10] Luther's spiritual distress was relieved by the insight of justification by faith in the context of a genuine penitence. The text Rom. 1:17 had confirmed that insight. In the glow of so great a deliverance, Luther seems to have been convinced that the Epistle of Paul to the Romans as a whole could only have meant to demonstrate the necessity of seeking salvation, his own salvation, along this path. The doctrine he had singled out in Paul, the one he had been looking for, was that of personal salvation. Once he had reached the end of the fifth chapter of

Romans, he accordingly felt he had come upon the extreme formulation of the apostle's thought. Professor Strohl ascribes to this restricted outlook a somewhat pessimistic undertone in Luther's religion. As he sees it in the light of all available primary sources, this religion at best amounted to a great consolation (*"getröstetes Elend"*), yet one suffused with the frustration of a man who had failed to experience in his Church the mighty, vivifying breath of the Spirit. Not so in the case of Paul whose genuine joy had found expression in a world conquering dynamism. How far apart, once one comes to think of it, the living organism of the Body of Christ exalted by Paul in Romans, chapters 12 to 15, and Luther's *communio sanctorum* exemplified by a small circle of friends! Luther had remained an individualist, and so it may be said of Protestantism in general that it also has remained far too individualistic.

What Luther's view of redemption may be said to have missed is the truth of redemption into the Kingdom of God through daily dying and rising again with Christ, and, at least to a certain degree, the Pauline experience of being possessed by a burning vision of hope and dynamic joy such as would defy the natural order. Hence we are left with a subsidiary, provincially individualistic view of salvation whose essential merits are that they are consoling and easily accessible to our Aristotelian logic.

Here, then, we have once more come to grips with anthropomorphic interpretation thriving close to the native shores of familiar experience. It has even been suggested by responsible interpreters that the one-sidedness of Luther owed more to those controversies about the Law which were so disturbing to Paul's humanity, than to the full Paulinian doctrine of redemption *per se*. Insofar as this may prove to have been the case, we seem to be confronted by a setback second to none in the history of Christianity. In the measure to which redemption is emphasized apart from faith in the Kingdom of God, a genuine sense of life and purpose has been lost, together with a longing and preparation for the Kingdom. Hearts have turned cold; human existence has become aimless and fruitless. Substitutes have appeared here and there as so many symptoms, mostly in the form of separatist movements, all of them witnessing to an incomplete, if not mutilated Christianity. While the proponents of the social gospel aimed at vindicating their one-sided Kingdom Christianity, they could not help exposing the moral sterility of the proponents of what amounted not only to justification, but to *salvation* by faith alone. Meanwhile, self-styled "evangelicals" exposed the activism of "liberals" guilty of substituting salvation through good works for salvation by faith alone.

In his admirable book, *The Mysticism of Paul the Apostle*— probably his best—Albert Schweitzer has laid his finger on the crux of the whole matter:

> So soon as Paulinism is made into any kind of doctrine of redemption, in which the concept of redemption is no longer attached to the kingdom of God, it naturally comes into opposition with the Gospel of Jesus, which is wholly oriented to the Kingdom of God. . . . An unauthentic Gospel of Jesus here comes into conflict with an unauthentic Gospel of Paul.[11]

Those seekers after mere "peace of mind" who would substitute a religion of their own making for the authentic, all-comprehensive Christian understanding of Paul had better keep away from the man of Lambaréné who has done the very opposite of this and has been willing to pay the cost. As Schweitzer sees it Christianity can keep its hold on successive generations only by being reconceived with the depth and comprehensiveness of the great apostle. To Paul we owe "the confidence that faith has nothing to fear from thinking, even when the latter disturbs its peace and raises a debate which appears to promise no good results for the religious

life." Schweitzer sums up the whole matter in the pungent assertion: "Paul vindicated for all time the rights of thought in
Christianity."[12]

The mysticism of Paul expresses the experience of a man forever unable to "kick against the pricks" of his God-given understanding. The quality of thinking it implies is at opposite poles
from that of wishful thinking. This is a fact which our age needs
to ponder on its way to a fresh recovery of purpose, especially if
that recovery is to prove secure. No amount of man-made truth
however clever, or even learned, can provide that security.

A genuine biblical experience and an adequate theological
understanding naturally issue in a glow of awareness. Any relevant
mental construct is bound to lend relevance to a whole range of
life. There is evidence of high thinking in certain propositions that
may at first strike one as commonplace. Thus Augustine could say
that God was more deeply within him than he himself. Nicolas
Berdyaev echoed this statement in the suggestion that one must
have the divine image in order to have the human image since
God is more truly human than man himself. What we have in
propositions such as these amounts to the quintessence of the
reverent thinking of a lifetime. There has hardly ever been a
genuine doctor of the Church who was not at the same time a
great saint, all silly epigrams on "foggy" mysticism notwithstanding. Sanctity which is health of spirit cannot safely ignore sanity
which is health of intellect. The recovery of Purpose with a capital
P is consummated at the apex where both come into their own in
the fullness of time.

The focus at which objectivation originates marks the point
where a man may fall or stand. Either his own understanding of
his mental constructs will ultimately testify to idolatrous departures
from God, or it will reveal the translucent Presence of the Originator within. The recovery of Purpose implies the restoration of this

translucent Presence in his person and mental picture. Not only does the experience provide perfect orientation, but it proves to be dynamic, uniquely power-giving. There is incalculable and unaccountable energy at work in it for the good of creation. The luminous transparence in which the living Truth is mediated calls forth the surrender of even a doubting Thomas: "My Lord and my God!" At this apex, the most concrete reality becomes known as one dwells upon it with ardor and fervor, thus coming into active relationship with the living God. The mystery of the Incarnate Word no longer is a problem, but rather has become an invitation to pilgrimage. The very word "purpose" loses its connotation of distant goal, once the "no longer I" has died on human lips in an almost face-to-face silent surrender.

At this upper edge of reality, a man's mood pertains to that of Dante at the end of *Paradiso:*

As is the geometer who wholly applies himself to measure the circle, and finds not by thinking that principle of which he is in need, such was I at that new sight. I wished to see how the image accorded with the circle, and how it has its place therein; but my own wings were not for this, had it not been that my mind was smitten by a flash in which its wish came.

To my high fantasy here power failed; but now my desire and my will, like a wheel which evenly is moved, the Love was turning which moves the Sun and the other stars.[13]

There are hallowed places where one wishes he could make an abiding tabernacle, unique moments when he prays it were in his power to suspend time, in the awareness that it is good for him to be where he is. Yet even Dante could not stay this ineffable Instant. Neither space nor time was in his power. The vision in itself was utterly past recall. What already mattered to him in his day, it would seem, was to restore to the living the true sense of purpose they had lost. The *Paradiso* in particular aimed at delivering from their state of wretchedness those who were dying in the midst of life and to point the way for them to the state of blessedness. The whole *Divine Comedy* was undertaken, not for the sake of speculation, but for a practical end. Whereupon Dante repaired to the world of men and affairs.

This truly is a great example to emulate, however distantly. He who has recovered the Vision owes it to his Crucified Lord to enlist in the Brotherhood of those who are heavy laden.

NOTES

INTRODUCTION

[1] *die Nachtansicht.* Cf. Gustav Theodor Fechner, *Die Tagenansicht gegenueber der Nachtansicht* (The Day View over against the Night View), 1879. Cf. new edition by Weizsaecker, Leipzig: Insel Verlag, 1923.

CHAPTER 1. THE DRAMA OF COSMIC PURPOSE

[1] *Macbeth*, Act V, sc. v.

[2] *The City of Dreadful Night*, XIX.

[3] Reprinted from *The Independent Review*, Dec. 1903, in *Mysticism and Logic and Other Essays*, New York: Longmans, Green and Co., 1918.

[4] Cambridge: Cambridge University Press, 1910–1913; v. I, 1910; v. II, 1912; v. III, 1913.

[5] Rufus Jones, *The Church's Debt to Heretics*, New York: Doran, 1924.

[6] *The Atlantic Monthly*, v. 182, 3 (Sept. 1948), 53–58. This quotation will be found on p. 54.

CHAPTER 2. TWILIGHT OF THE FINAL CAUSE

[1] *A History of the Warfare of Science with Theology in Christendom* (1895) is now available in one volume, New York: George Braziller, 1955.

[2] Cf. Max Planck, *The Philosophy of Physics*, New York: W. W. Norton & Co., 1936, II "Causality in Nature," pp. 82, 83.

[3] See especially, *Les Étapes de la Pensée Mathématique*, Paris: P.U.F., 1912; *L'Expérience Humaine de la Causalité Physique*, Paris: P.U.F., 1922; also "Le Déterminisme et la Causalité dans la Physique Contemporaine," in *Bulletin de la Société Française de Philosophie*, 1930, 3, 51–71.

CHAPTER 3. THE WAY OF MENTAL CONSTRUCTION

[1] British edition, Oxford: Basil Blackwell, 1951. American edition, New York: Harcourt, Brace & Co., 1952.

[2] German original, pp. 163–67; English translation, pp. 157–62 of the American edition.

[3] P. 158.

4 Idem.

5 Idem.

6 Cf. Hans Vaihinger, *Philosophie des Als Ob*, 1911; *The Philosophy of "As if,"* translated by C. K. Ogden, London: Kegan Paul, 1924.

CHAPTER 4. THE IMPACT OF SCIENTIFIC METHODS

1 Sigmund Freud, *A General Introduction to Psycho-Analysis*, Garden City, New York: Doubleday & Co. Permabooks, 1953, Fifteenth Lecture, p. 248.

2 Cf. Einstein:

"As to those who regard contemporary quantum theory as a piece of knowledge which is final in principle, they waver in fact between two possible interpretations, namely,

"1. There is a physical reality. Its laws, however, do not allow of any other than statistical expression.

"2. There is nothing at all which corresponds to a physical situation. Merely possibilities 'exist' and may be observed.

"We both agree on this point: we regard these two interpretations with disbelief and we believe in the possibility of a theory which is able to give a complete description of reality, the laws of which establish relations between the things themselves and not merely between their probabilities." (Letter from Dr. Albert Einstein to Lord Herbert L. Samuel, dated Princeton, N.J., October 13, 1950, in Herbert L. Samuel's *Essays in Physics*, New York: Harcourt, Brace & Co., 1952, p. 161.)

3 I would remind the reader that *A Free Man's Worship* was originally published in *The Independent Review* of December 1903. The "birthday" of the quantum theory may be said to have been December 14, 1900, when Max Planck reported before the Physical Society of Berlin the finding relating to his constant, *k*. This finding contained the introduction of the ultimate energy quanta. On this see Max Planck's own dramatic report in his *Scientific Autobiography and other Papers*, New York: Philosophical Library, 1949, esp. p. 42. On the other hand, the Heisenberg principle of indeterminacy was only announced in 1927. Hence my wording, "in part originated, and in part later vindicated."

CHAPTER 5. A MATTER OF PROPER JURISDICTION

1 Pascal, Pensées, fr. 72, in *Oeuvres* publiées par Léon Brunschvicg, Paris: Hachette, 1921, v. 12, 73, 74.

2 Albert Schweitzer, Epilogue to *The Theology of Albert Schweitzer for Christian Inquirers*, by E. N. Mozley, New York: Macmillan, 1950, p. 114.

CHAPTER 6. PRELIMINARY WORDS OF CAUTION

1 "I'm With You Once Again," stanza 3.

Chapter 7. A Record Contrary to Expectation

[1] *Collected Papers of Evelyn Underhill,* edited by Lucy Menzies, New York. Longmans, Green and Co., 1946, pp. 182, 183.

Chapter 8. A Misplaced Rationalism Exposed

[1] A. N. Whitehead, *Science and the Modern World,* New York: Macmillan, 1925, p. 12.

[2] *Republic,* II, 362–67.

[3] See esp. VI, 509–VII (which begins with the famous parable of the Cave or Den), 514–20.

[4] Cf. Gaunilo's *Pro Insipiente,* the defense of the "Fool," and Anselm's *Apology in Reply to Gaunilon,* translated by S. N. Deane, 1903.

Chapter 9. The Barthian Critique of Schleiermacher

[1] "The name of Schleiermacher belongs and for all time will belong at the summit of the theology of recent times, with none beside him" (p. 379).

[2] For two representative passages see *The Doctrine of the Word of God* (translated by G. T. Thomson), pp. 218–83, and *Kirchliche Dogmatik,* III, 2, 23 ff.

[3] For the Barthian critique of Descartes see esp. *KD,* III, 1, 401–15. Cf. also excellent study of Robert E. Cushman, "Barth's Attack upon Cartesianism and the Future in Theology," in *The Journal of Religion,* v. 36, 4 (October 1956), 207–23.

[4] Cf. *The Doctrine of the Word of God,* pp. 21, 22, and *KD,* III, 2, 134 ff., where Barth draws freely upon Jaspers for his critique of existentialism.

[5] Cf. Schleiermacher's *Discourses on Religion,* esp. his "Second Discourse" on the nature of religion, with special attention to his conception of God toward the close, in the second edition (1821). All editions thereafter are reprints.

[6] *KD,* III, 2, 29–35.

[7] *KD,* III, 2, 47–63, and entire section 44, "Man as God's Creature," 64–241 (as contrasted to the Phenomenal Man who is not the real man at all).

[8] *KD,* III, 2, 22–27.
See also Barth's lecture *Evangelium und Bildung,* and his *KD,* I, 2, 516 ff. for a presentation of a Christian program of culture from the standpoint of the knowledge of Christ through faith.

Chapter 10. A Common Indictment of Anthropomorphism

[1] R. H. Lightfoot, *History and Interpretation in the Gospels,* New York: Harper & Brothers, 1935, p. 225.

[2] *KD,* I, 11, 77–113; *Credo,* 8. *Passus sub Pontio Pilato,* pp. 66–74.

[3] *KD,* I, 11, 71; *The Doctrine of the Word of God,* 124–35; 457–512.

[4] Emil Brunner, *Revelation and Reason,* Philadelphia: The Westminster Press, 1946, p. 383.

CHAPTER 11. THE WIDER MEANING OF REVELATION

[1] Bronislaw Malinowski, art. "Culture" in *Encyclopedia of Social Sciences,* v. 4, 621 ff.

[2] Consult the authorized English translation, *Manifesto of the Communist Party* by Karl Marx and Friedrich Engels, New York: International Publishers, 1932.

[3] William Temple, *Nature, Man and God,* New York: Macmillan, pp. 9, 10.

CHAPTER 12. REVELATION AND DEGREES OF RESPONSE

[1] James H. Breasted, *The Dawn of Conscience,* The Sources of our Moral Heritage in the Ancient World, New York: Scribner's, 1933, pp. 160, 161.

[2] Charles Hartshorne, *The Divine Relativity,* a Social Conception of God, New Haven: Yale University Press, 1948, pp. 48, 49.

[3] Herman Melville, *Moby Dick,* ch. 18, "His Mark."

[4] *Ibid.,* ch. 41, "Moby Dick."

[5] Albert Schweitzer, *Out of My Life and Thought,* An Autobiography, New York: Henry Holt & Co., 1933, 1949, pp. 232–33.

[6] Albert Schweitzer, *The Quest of the Historical Jesus,* A Critical Study of its Progress from Reimarus to Wrede, New York: Macmillan, 1955, p. 403.

[7] *Out of My Life and Thought,* p. 156.

CHAPTER 13. CUTTING ACROSS ESTABLISHED VIEWS

[1] J. S. Whale, *Christian Doctrine,* New York: Macmillan, 1941, p. 57.

[2] On the idea of *felix culpa* see *The Tragic Vision and the Christian Faith,* ed. by Nathan A. Scott, Jr., New York: Association Press, ch. 1, by Edmond LaB. Cherbonnier, pp. 50, 51.

[3] A scholarly treatment of Milton's heterodoxies with special attention to his *De Doctrina Christiana* will be found in *Biblical Criticism and Heresy in Milton,* by George N. Conklin, New York: King's Crown Press, Columbia University, 1949.

CHAPTER 14. CUTTING ACROSS ESTABLISHED VIEWS (continued)

[1] *The Tragic Vision of the Christian Faith,* ed. by Nathan A. Scott, Jr., ch. 1, "Biblical Faith and the Idea of Tragedy" by Edmond LaB. Cherbonnier, p. 40. This whole chapter is most illuminating. Not only do I find myself in agreement with the author, but I gladly acknowledge my debt to him for precious insights.

[2] *Inferno,* Canto XXXIV. This passage was kindly translated for me by my late colleague and friend, Professor George Franklin Cole, of the University of Pennsylvania.

[3] Denzil G. M. Patrick, *Pascal and Kierkegaard,* London and Redhill: Lutterworth Press, 1947, v. 2, 385.

CHAPTER 15.   DOOM OR DESTINY

[1] *On the Prescription against Heretics,* 7.

[2] *Divine Institutes,* 1, 5.

[3] *Letters,* 22, 29.

[4] *On Belief in the Resurrection,* II, 86.

[5] For essential passages in the most accessible presentation by Kant, see *Prolegomena to Any Future Metaphysics,* Conclusion, § 57, § 59, and "Solution of the general question of the *Prolegomena,* How is metaphysics possible as a science?"

[6] Bertrand Russell has made an impressive pronouncement on this:
"When this check upon pride is removed, a further step is taken on the road towards a certain kind of madness—the intoxication of power which invaded philosophy with Fichte, and to which modern men, whether philosophers or not, are prone. I am persuaded that this intoxication of power is the greatest danger of our time, and that any philosophy which, however unintentionally, contributes to it is increasing the danger of vast social disaster." *A History of Western Philosophy,* New York: Simon and Schuster, 1945, p. 828.

CHAPTER 16.   EGO OR PURPOSE

[1] It is noteworthy that Karl Barth has singled out Fichte and Feuerbach side by side with Schleiermacher in his critique of the anthropological approach. In the case of Fichte, see *KD,* 2, 110, 111. In the case of Feuerbach, see *Die Theologie und die Kirche,* essay on "Ludwig Feuerbach," pp. 212–39.

[2] Gerald Heard, *The Eternal Gospel,* New York: Harper, 1946, p. 214.

[3] *The Saturday Review,* March 15, 1947, p. 14.

[4] Alfred North Whitehead, *Science and the Modern World,* Lowell Lectures, 1925, New York: Macmillan, 1925, pp. 15, 16.

[5] George S. Hendry, *The Holy Spirit in Christian Theology,* Philadelphia: The Westminster Press, 1956, p. 117.

CONCLUSION

[1] This same need has recently been acknowledged by William Ernest Hocking in *The Coming World Civilization,* New York: Harper, 1956. Although Professor Hocking's thesis leaves far behind Christian positions I deem essential, I welcome this opportunity to pay a tribute of gratitude to a great soul and to a brave book.

The recovery of purpose has educational implications of great importance. Such however are the scope and special character of the problems involved, that they call for an independent study. A rich documentation on the subject may be found in Frank E. Gaebelein's *Christian Education in a Democracy,* New York: Oxford University Press, 1951. I agree with the author that a refusal on the part of secular education "to see beyond this world, coupled with its disinterest in eternal values, inevitably limits not only its content but also its product" (p. 260).

2 *Lucifer and Prometheus,* London: Routledge and Kegan Paul, 1952.

3 Henrik Ibsen, *A Doll's House,* Act II.

4 *Puritan Sage,* Collected Writings of Jonathan Edwards, ed. by Vergilius Ferm, New York: Library Publishers, 1953, pp. 377, 378.

5 In his Epilogue to E. N. Mozley's *The Theology of Albert Schweitzer for Christian Inquirers,* p. 97.

6 On this see *The Riddle of The New Testament* by E. Hoskyns and N. Davey, London: Faber and Faber, 1931, p. 124.

7 Paul Sevier Minear, *Eyes of Faith,* A Study of the Biblical Point of View, Philadelphia: The Westminster Press, 1946, p. 2.

8 D. M. Baillie, *God Was in Christ,* New York: Charles Scribner's Sons, 1948, p. 47.

9 *Ibid.,* p. 53.

10 Cf. Henri Strohl, *L'Épanouissement de la Pensée de Luther,* Strasbourg: Istra, 1924, esp. I, ch. 6, § 3, "Luther et le Paulinisme," pp. 104–13.

11 Albert Schweitzer, *The Mysticism of Paul the Apostle* (1931), New York: Macmillan, 1955, pp. 392, 393.

12 *Ibid.,* p. 376.

13 *The Divine Comedy of Dante Alighieri,* translated by Charles Eliot Norton, III, *Paradise,* Boston and New York: Houghton, Mifflin, The Riverside Press, Cambridge, 1893, 214, 215.

The fragment here quoted is the end of Canto 33 in *Paradiso,* and concludes *The Divine Comedy.*

INDEX